Generation to Generation

Generation to Generation

Personal Recollections of a Chassidic Legacy

Abraham J. Twerski

TRADITIONAL PRESS, INC.
Brooklyn, New York

A CIS PUBLICATION

First published by:
Traditional Press
Brooklyn, New York

Published and Distributed by:
C.I.S. Publishers and Distributors
180 Park Avenue, Lakewood, New Jersey 08701
(201)905-3000/1 Fax: (201) 367-6666

Distributed in Israel by:
C.I.S. International (Israel)
Rechov Mishkalov 18/16, Har Nof, Jerusalem
Tel: 02-538-935

Distributed in the U.K. and Europe by:
C.I.S. International (U.K.)
1 Palm Court, Queen Elizabeth Walk
London, England N16
Tel: 01-809-3723

ISBN 0-933711-17-4

Library of Congress Cataloging in Publication Data

Twerski, Abraham J.
Generation to Generation

1. Lengends, Hasidic, 2. Jewish way of life.
3. Twerski, Abraham J.—Childhood and youth. I. Title.
BM532.T94 286.8′33 86-1309

PRINTED IN THE UNITED STATES OF AMERICA

Table of Contents

I

Introduction

We were sitting at a *Shabbos* meal. I was relating to our guest some of the many stories that had been handed down in my family, and sharing with him a few of my memories of first-generation American Jews. I mentioned to our guest how upset I had been with my uncle, who had been a virtual treasure-house of family traditions and stories laden with precious teachings, and who had committed only a small fraction of these to writing and took the rest of them with him to eternity.

"You are critical of your uncle," our guest said, "but aren't you guilty of the same thing?"

I could not help but realize that my friend was right. Even with all the wisdom that has been preserved in rabbinic and folk writings throughout the historic ages, far too much has been permitted to be lost to posterity.

I have therefore recorded a number of the stories and anecdotes that I could recall. Among these are reminiscences of people I knew in my childhood, a generation that will never be duplicated, and which should be preserved historically. There are also chassidic stories, most of which I heard from my father. I have also included some personal experiences, as well as a few folk tales.

Although much of the material in this book will be new to the reader, some of the chassidic stories and folk tales may have appeared in print elsewhere. Nevertheless, I have taken the liberty of repeating some stories because of the interpretations that were given to them by my father or that I have inferred. I believe that Father never told a story unless it conveyed some practical teaching, and it is the latter that I hope to transmit.

As the anecdotes fell together, they appeared to follow a theme. Some attest to the good within oneself, some to the good in another person, and others to the good that exists in a world that so often appears cruel and hostile. Thus the majority of stories provide cause for a more positive and optimistic attitude toward life.

Some of the anecdotes relate to Milwaukee, where I was born and spent the first three decades of my life. The Jewish community of Milwaukee was comprised largely of Russian and German immigrants. A few of these people had achieved some Jewish learning in the old country, but many who came to the United States as youngsters became involved immediately in the struggle for survival, and did not have an opportunity to further their Jewish learning.

As in many other American cities, the Orthodox immigrants maintained the traditions and practices of their parents, and tried to preserve these values in their homes. However, they generally did not provide adequate Jewish education for their children, who were often accorded nothing more than after-school Talmud Torah classes.

My father settled in Milwaukee in 1927, and was the chassidic Rebbe of the city. He began with a nucleus of Ukranian *landsleit* (countrymen) but gradually achieved a following among all segments of the community. He was a counselor to countless individuals and families, and when I was a child, I could not help but overhear many of the proceedings in his study. In addition, our *Shabbos* table was always graced by many guests, some of whom were itinerant rabbis, and I would hear Father in his Torah discussions with them, or perhaps relating a parable or a chassidic story. These are the sources of my material.

This book contains a collection of anecdotes which do not lend themselves to neat categorizations, but I have nevertheless tried to organize the material under several topic headings.

If the material presented herein proves to be at least half as instructive and enjoyable to the reader as it has been to me, this effort will have been well worthwhile.

II

The Value Of Memories

Give diamonds, because a diamond is forever. So says the ad, but this is not quite true.

Yes, a diamond is indeed most durable, the hardest substance known to man, but as a possession, it is hardly eternal. It can be lost or stolen, leaving one only with the grief over its loss.

If you wish to give a gift which is truly forever, give memories.

I was not fully aware of the durability and value of memories until the following incident:

I had just completed a presentation of medical uses of hypnosis to a group of physicians, in which hypnotic anesthesia was rather dramatically demonstrated, when a doctor approached me saying, "You've got to see a patient for me."

Morris was a man in his fifties. He had undergone surgery for cancer but unfortunately had a recurrence. He was having a great deal of pain, but avoided strong pain-killing medication because it clouded his thinking.

"Morris is a wonderful man, who has been a pillar of strength to the community and has helped countless individuals. He deserves every bit of help. I can't give him any more," the doctor said. "You can, and you are going to."

Morris had always been an active person. His time had been equally divided between his business and the many community projects in which he was active. All this had changed with the advent of the pain, which had made even walking difficult. He did not go to the business or to his community meetings. Some days he needed a wheel chair just to get around the house. He had quite understandably become depressed.

My efforts at getting Morris into a hypnotic trance sufficient to produce pain relief were unsuccessful. In an attempt to deepen the light trance he had entered, I suggested that he allow himself to go back in time and recall some pleasant experiences.

Under hypnosis, Morris began relating that he was riding his bike on a country road. He was now just 13, and had received a new bike for his Bar Mitzvah. What is now a built-up suburb was then open farmland, and on Sunday morning after completing his paper route, he would ride around the countryside, fully enjoying his new bike.

Morris seemed to have enjoyed this session, so several days later I had him repeat it. This time, he was biking together with a few friends, all of whom he recalled by name. After he awoke from this bike-ride trance, he said, "I am getting hungry." Morris had not had any appetite for many weeks.

I continued to use this technique of trying to deepen the trance by having Morris relive enjoyable experiences. He obviously enjoyed the trances, but I could never get him into a trance depth adequate for pain removal. I then called his physician to report my lack of success, but before I could say anything he said, "Thanks so much for what you are doing for Morris. Esther is just ecstatic about his recovery."

Curious, I called Esther, who was beside herself with gratitude. "Morris is a new person," she said. "He has been to the office a few times. Sunday morning, he even drove himself to the *shul* for the men's club minyan. He so looks forward to his sessions with you."

I wasn't quite sure what to make of this, but since something beneficial was obviously happening, I continued the trances. I then instructed Morris how to do self-hynosis. Twice or three times every day, he would relax and go into a trance, re-experiencing some enjoyable event of the past. There proved to be many of these. He remembered a loving grandfather, with a long white beard which he loved to stroke. When he was a child, he would accompany his grandfather to *shul* on Friday night and get a taste of the sweet wine when the cantor said the *Kiddush*. He recalled family picnics and outings in the park. He re-lived going on boat rides and to baseball games with his father. He re-experienced trips to Israel and vacations with his family. But most often there were the long bike rides, alone or with friends.

Morris continued to be active, although the cancer was continuing its relentless course. One time, I visited him in the hospital when he relapsed, and he said he was so happy to see me. The administration of intravenous fluids was interfering with his ability to go into a trance, and would I help him a bit? Within a few minutes, he was off bike-riding.

Morris died peacefully, having been active almost to the end. Although I had never been able to achieve hypnotic anesthesia with him, he had hardly ever complained of pain.

Why had Morris improved so dramatically with the trances? The answer eventually became apparent to me.

It had never occurred to me before that what keeps most of us going is the anticipation of the future. We are always looking forward to something good happening. We look forward to an enjoyable vacation, or to a relaxing weekend. We look forward to enjoying our children's successes, and to the *nachas* of our grandchildren. We always invariably look forward with the expectation of something pleasant.

What, then, happens to a person when he realizes that he has a disease which will increasingly prevent him from enjoying things? What happens when he understands that for him, there is no future? I believe that this results in a total loss of motivation, in withdrawal from activities of everyday life, and in depression. When a person feels this way, any physical pain he suffers must be magnified a thousand fold.

Morris was fortunate to find a new way to enjoy life. Filed away within our billions of brain cells are the memories of virtually everthing we have ever experienced. If only we could find the key to those files and retrieve those memories! Morris found that key. He knew that all he had to do was to recline in an easy chair, let himself drift into a trance, and set the clock back to some enjoyable experience which he could relive. He actually looked forward to getting up in the morning, because it meant that he had a full day to relive several more enjoyable episodes. During the last year of his life, Morris relived over fifty years.

Morris taught me a great deal. Even those of us who are fortunate in having a future to anticipate need not allow the past to be lost and forgotten. Whether we use hypnosis, a diary, a photo album, or whether we just share the stories of pleasant events with one another, we can enrich our lives by recapturing and reliving enjoyable moments.

One does not have to be, God forbid, sick in order to enjoy memories. Nor is it essential to undergo hypnosis to retrieve them. I'm sure you have pleasant memories which you can recall. Perhaps you might like to share some of my favorite ones.

III

Raised In My Father's Home

"*Lebedig, kinderlach, lebedig*!" ("Lively, my children, be lively!") was Father's most frequent admonition. "*Kinderlach*" was a term which he used for all his followers, and was not restricted to his biological children. Indeed, Father exuded a spirit of joy with his very presence. It is of interest that anyone speaking of him today invariably smiles. Even his memory is comforting and refreshing.

His exhilarating charisma was actually one of the reasons I left the rabbinate to enter medicine. Father had a practice of frequently visiting all of the local hospitals to comfort his congregants and acquaintances who were patients there. After my ordination, when I became Father's assistant, I suggested to him that I could lighten his load by alternating days of hospital rounds with him, to which he readily agreed. He would then tell me whom I was to visit.

One day I walked into a patient's room, and after chatting with the patient for a few minutes, the latter said, "You know, Rabbi, your father was here yesterday. I had been in terrible pain all day, and nothing the doctors had given me for pain was working. Then your father walked in, and as if by magic, the pain was gone."

I left that room knowing that this was an act I could not possibly follow.

There is one beautiful photograph we have of Father, in which he has a very stern expression. Mother swears that this must have been trick photography, because in fifty-some years of marriage, she had never seen him with a stern expression.

It was a trick, all right, but the trick was not in the photography. Rather, it was in Father's skill in never letting this sternness be communicated in pure culture.

Father's sternness was essential, for otherwise we would have grown up to be spoiled adults as well as spoiled children. However, just as some vital ingredients in a dish are never tasted as such, but make their presence felt by their effects on the other ingredients, so Father's sternness was there, but never identifiable.

Father's personality and demeanor represented to me what chassidic Jewishness was all about: a pervasive, persistent, and contagious attitude of *simcha* (joy) which was not at all incompatible with some of the harsh realities of life, nor with the restraints, deprivations, and even distress encountered in coping with these realities. In fact, it was precisely when spirits were low that the revitalizing charge was heard: "*Lebedig, kinderlach, lebedig*!"

One of the major teachings of chassidus is that *simcha,* joy, must be achieved at all costs.

There is far too much suffering in the world. Too much disease, too many accidents, too many so-called "acts of fate" that cause misery and grief. Young children are stricken, young lives and families are devastated. Why? Why?

Science has failed to provide answers, and wise philosophers shrug their shoulders. People turn to theologians, those who are supposed to convey the Divine wisdom, to explain the rationale of suffering.

We read and analyze the Book of Job. We have many good questions, but no satisfactory answers. Little wonder. The Midrash tells us that in a direct conversation with God, Moses asked this very question, "Why do terrible things happen to good people?" And God replied, "This is something you cannot grasp as long as you reside in a physical body. No living person can understand this mystery. Even you, Moses, who have been privy to many Divine secrets, will have to wait until the after-life to understand this."

The Talmud requires a faith and trust in God so great, that a person should actually express gratitude to God for the bad things that befall him, as well as for the good things in life.

A follower of the great chassidic master, the Maggid of Mezeritch, once posed this question to him. "How can the Talmud make such a superhuman demand of a person? How can it be expected that a person will be grateful for the bad things he experiences?"

The Maggid referred the man to Rebbe Zusia. Whereas all the Maggid's disciples were great scholars, and no less a Talmudic authority than Rebbe Shneur Zalman referred to Rebbe Zusia as the "true gaon" (Talmudic genius), Rebbe Zusia took great pains to keep his scholarship well-concealed. He would do his learning secretly, and never permitted anyone to observe him studying Torah. Incidentally, Rebbe Zusia was the victim of several very painful diseases, and his suffering was much aggravated by his extreme poverty.

When the man approached Rebbe Zusia with his question, the latter told him that there had certainly been some mistake, that he must not have heard correctly. "Everyone knows I am ignorant of learning," he said. "I know nothing about the Talmud. The Maggid must have directed you to someone else."

The man insisted that he had not been mistaken, and was adamant in posing the question to him, which he eventually did. "You see," said Rebbe Zusia, "that just proves that you are mistaken. How could I be expected to explain how one can be grateful for bad things that occur, when I have never had the experience of anything bad happening to me?"

The man looked at Rebbe Zusia, who was weak with hunger, racked with pain, and clad in tattered clothes, and understood the answer to his question.

It is widely assumed that *simcha* is incompatible with suffering. Chassidus reconciled the two. A child who truly knows how intensely his father loves him, and has the intelligence to understand that his father's intentions are solely and exclusively for the child's welfare, would always be grateful for what his father does *to* him as well as for him, even if he experiences this as distressing and painful.

When we are in anguish, we cry to the Almighty for help. Rebbe Boruch of Medziboz cited the Talmud, that the "gates of tears are never locked." "Why, then," asked Rebbe Boruch, "is there a need for a gate if it is never to be closed?"

Rebbe Boruch answered, "The gate is there to be closed when one cries unwisely. When one prays for something which is in fact to his own disadvantage, the gates are then shut."

A philosopher once questioned a Rebbe about how a just God could permit injustices to happen.

The Rebbe turned the discussion around to one of the philosopher's theories, and challenged it with a cogent argument. The philosopher was able to refute the argument and defend the validity of his theory. The Rebbe then hurled another challenge, which the philosopher again rebuffed. So the discussion continued with the philosopher successfully fending off every challenge.

Finally, the Rebbe said, "If you had exerted as much effort in rebuffing your challenges against Divine wisdom as you do for challenges against your theory, you would have no complaints about God's management of the world." Acceptance of Divine wisdom as just not only makes the world tolerable, but even enjoyable.

The Baal Shem Tov, the founder of chassidism, came upon the scene in the seventeenth century, wherein the Jews of eastern Europe were in profound depression. They had just witnessed the bloody pogroms of 1647-1649, and still felt their lives to be in jeopardy. Deprived of basic civil rights and the freedom to engage in commerce, poverty was rampant. Relatively few Jews had achieved much Torah study, which could have sustained their spirits. Some of the Torah scholars looked upon the unlearned populace with deflating condescension. Finally, the bitter disillusionment following in the wake of Sabbatai Zevi, the false messiah, dashed the messianic hope for many Jews.

It was to these people that the Baal Shem Tov brought his teachings of hope and joy. True, he explained, the suffering is great, but the ultimate benevolence of God is not to be doubted, and in His infinite and unfathomable wisdom, there is purpose to this suffering. Man must never forget that he is the crown jewel, the ultimate object of creation, and the Jew must never forget that he has a unique mission in bringing Godliness and *kedusha* (holiness) into the terrestrial world. This mission is accomplished when the Jew fulfills the Divine *mitzvohs* (commandments) to the best of one's capacities. Hence, the sincere devotion of the unlearned Jew, who puts his entire heart into his prayers and good deeds, is as dear to God as the service of the most eminent scholar.

Indeed, when a Jew rushes home late in the day after hours of hard labor, and discovering that there are but moments until sunset, hurriedly recites the *Mincha* (afternoon service) with fear lest he forfeit the prayer by tardiness, "Know ye," said the Baal Shem Tov, "that the heavenly host tremble before the *kedusha* of this prayer." In fulfilling the Divine commandments to the best of one's capability, one comes into a close relationship with God, and this should provide ample reason for *simcha*.

⸙

Even the distress of remorse should not extinguish *simcha*.

Remorse over one's mistakes is essential, as is mourning over the Divine displacement from the sanctuary in Jerusalem and the exile of Israel. But these need not and dare not lead to sadness.

That mourning and joy are not mutually exclusive was made evident to me at the *kotel* (the western wall), where on my first visit on a Thursday, I tore my garment according to the *halachic* (Jewish law) regulation as an expression of sorrow. On the following night at the *Shabbos* eve services at the *kotel,* we joined hands and danced in jubilation in welcoming the *Shabbos* Queen. I recall thinking, is this a site for sorrow or a site for joy? The answer, of course, is that it is a site for both. This must have been the intent of the Rebbe of Ropsicz who used to say that *simcha* must be so pervasive, that even when mourning is called for, one must learn how to mourn with joy. Similarly, the remorse, self-castigation, and humility that is required of the Jew need not result in sadness.

The great Rebbe of Karlin carefully distinguished the feeling of humility, of recognizing that one has not yet begun to achieve his mission on earth, from that of depression, of feeling worthless and in despair. The former is constructive, since it stimulates one to action and to accomplishment, whereas the latter leads to lethargy, to resignation and surrender out of hopelessness.

The Rebbe further explained that humility and depression are not only dissimilar, but are actually polar opposites. For what is dejection but the accumulation of many disappointments and dissatisfactions, with many personal needs being unmet? A person who was truly humble would not have such disappointments because in his humility, he would not feel that he was deserving of all these things in the first place. Self-effacement in the presence of God is the key. If you *are* nothing, you cannot want for anything.

This nothingness of humility is totally different from the worthlessness of depression. It is the nothingness of the glow of a lit match held against the blazing sun, wherein the small flame is indiscernible because of the sun's great brightness. It is the effacement of man in the presence of God. Indeed one can feel proud and privileged that such a "nothing" has been commissioned by the Sovereign of the entire universe to fulfill a mission. One rejoices with this honor, and seeks to be worthy of it.

Thus, even at those times in life when circumstances give little reason for joy, there is nevertheless reason for being joyous. Perhaps we can understand joy by contrasting it with its opposite, the distress of grief. Father often told the story of a man who had been sentenced to twenty-five years of hard labor. He was shackled to the handle of an immense, heavy wheel built into a wall, and from morning to night he had to turn this heavy wheel. The days and years passed slowly, and during these many hours, as he felt his muscles growing weary and the bones of his back breaking under the stress, he would wonder just what it was he was accomplishing with his hard work. Perhaps the wheel was part of a mill, and he was grinding grain into flour. Or perhaps he was rotating something like a potter's wheel, or maybe generating some kind of energy that was being used to activate some type of machine.

When the long, long sentence was finally completed, and the shackles were removed from the sinewy arms of a broken, old man, the first thing the latter did was to go around to the outside of the wall to see what it was that he had been laboring at for these twenty-five years. To his horror he discovered that there was nothing there, just a wheel in the wall, unattached to any lever or any gear.

The man broke down in sobs. "Twenty-five years of hard labor," he wailed, "and all for nothing. Had anyone benefited from it, be it man or beast, I could have accepted it. But to have worked and suffered for nothing at all, this is unbearable!"

There can be no more profound distress or disappointment than for one's life to be pointless. All our travails can be taken in stride if only there is a purpose to all of this. But if, as some scientific philosophers would have us believe, we are accidents of chance, with no ultimate purpose to our being, then the tragedies of life become unbearable.

Just as a sense of purposelessness is the nadir of despair, so is an awareness of purposefulness the pinnacle of joy. Everything is for a reason, everything is for a purpose. There is joy in accomplishment. The woman who suffers the pangs of labor may indeed cry out with pain, but the pain is mitigated by her knowledge that she is gaining a child, and if she wishes to have more children, she does so with the full knowledge of the pain that she will endure. The anticipation of the ultimate joy of raising a child enables her to joyfully exclaim, "Mazel Tov!" even while the pain-induced tears roll down her cheeks.

So, "*Lebedig, kinderlach, lebedig*!" It's all worthwhile. Everything.

⁂

Perhaps the greatest single challenge facing parents is to raise their children with values, with the knowledge of what is right and wrong, and with the desire to do that which is right and avoid doing wrong, while at the same time promoting the development of a positive self-concept and not making the child feel that he is bad if he has done something wrong.

This requires discipline, and discipline demands that a child be made aware that some things that he has done, does, or wishes to do are unacceptable and not permissible. But how does one do this without making the child feel that he is somehow bad or guilty?

I would like to share with you a childhood recollection. One of the few memories that I have of being disciplined by my father for something of which he disapproved, was of his telling me in a quiet, firm, and no-nonsense tone, "*Es past nisht!*"(This does not become you!)

The message was clear. I knew what it was that I was not to do. But it was not until many years later that I appreciated the full content of Father's rebuke. He had told me that I was not to do something because that particular behavior was beneath me. "*Es past nisht*" meant that I was too good for that. This is the diametric opposite of a put-down. I was told that I was a person of excellence. There was no mention that what I was doing was inherently wrong or bad, but the emphasis was rather on me. I was above such behavior. This is incompatible, Father told me, out of character for someone like yourself.

Today, I sit in my office, and a young man or woman of sixteen or seventeen is brought in for treatment of a drug abuse problem. Questioning elicits that for several years this beautiful child has been putting these harmful substances into his/her body.

"Tell me," I ask. "What do you do if you are working in the kitchen and accumulate garbage? Where do you put the garbage?"

Invariably there is a puzzled look. "Why, in the garbage pail, of course. Where else?"

"Then tell me, my child, how is it that you have been putting all this drug garbage into yourself? I'm sure you knew this stuff you were taking was all garbage, didn't you?"

It has never yet failed. Usually the tears well up, and these lovely children tell me that they had *never* felt good about themselves. Essentially, they saw nothing inappropriate in introducing garbage into their systems, because their perception of themselves was distorted and deflated. They thought of themselves as trash cans.

How different would people be if they knew that certain types of behavior are proscribed because "*Es past nisht*!" Every child can understand that when you are dressed in your finest garments, you do not engage in activities which might soil them. Some things are just too fine and precious to be exposed to the risk of being soiled or damaged.

My father never read any psychological works on correct parenting. Undoubtedly, he too had been told, "*Es past nisht*," as had his father and grandfather before him, all the way back to the gathering at Sinai, when a people just weeks away from decades of enslavement that broke the body and crushed the spirit were told, "You shall be unto Me a kingdom of priests and sacred people." Then they were given a list of practices from which they must abstain for one overriding reason: "*Es past nisht*."

⸙

I claim no expertise in child psychology, but I must take issue with those who say that indulging a child invariably leads to serious problems in later life. I was copiously indulged, and turned out to have relatively few emotional hang-ups (or so I like to think). It is only *unbalanced* indulgence that is destructive; indulgence not counterbalanced by a sense of responsibility and a demand for compliance with certain standards of behavior.

Indulgence which takes the form of giving the child deserved recognition is certainly not harmful. In fact, it is the absence of demonstration of appreciation of the child's assets that leads to problems, especially with development of low self-esteem.

I can recall many times when I was praised by Father, and when I merited it, he let me know how proud he was of me.

As a young child, I liked to blow the *shofar* (ram's horn), and Father gave me a little *shofar* which was my very own. I became quite proficient in its use.

One Rosh Hoshanah during the *amidah* (the silent service), at the point when the *shofar* was to be sounded, I saw that the man assigned to this task was having troubles. He could not get a sound out of the *shofar*. After a few attempts, he passed the *shofar* down to another worshipper, whose efforts were no more successful than the first. The *shofar* was passed around the congregation, all to no avail. Apparently Satan had gotten into the *shofar* and was obstructing the sound.

I figured that this had gone far enough. I took out my little *shofar*, and blew all the required sounds. The congregation resumed the *amidah*, and at the next designated point, everyone assumed that whoever had successfully blown the *shofar* would do so again, which I did. I completed all three soundings during the *amidah*. The worshippers, who wore their *talesim* (prayer shawls) over their heads to prevent distraction, could see nothing.

After the service, when it was discovered that the *shofar* had been blown by an eight-year-old, Father ruled that all the soundings had to be repeated by someone of age, since a minor was not permitted to sound the *shofar*. But Father's glee was without bounds. He thoroughly enjoyed my performance, and when any itinerant rabbis visited, he never failed to tell of the stunt that I had performed.

Father took great pride in almost everything I did, and did

not hesitate to boast of these to others in my presence. Yet the firmness in his insistence on appropriate behavior (*"Es past nisht"*), and the inherent message, "To the degree to which you have been endowed with personality assets, to that degree you are accountable for performance," converted all the pleasant strokes into stern demands for responsible behavior. The ingredients for self-esteem were thus not permitted to run away into grandiosity.

I have a memory of an encounter with a local rabbi as a small child. The rabbi explained that the Talmud sometimes equates thought with deed. "Now if thinking is like acting," he said, "I am thinking of a question, which is equivalent to the act of verbalizing the question. So you should give me the answer to the question that I am now thinking."

I responded with what appeared to be the only logical reply. "I am thinking of the answer," I said.

The rabbi ran in to tell Father what he considered to be an exceptionally bright response and said, "Some day he will be a great scholar," to which Father readily agreed. I regret that I have not fulfilled their aspirations. The important point is that here, too, any praise given was accompanied by a demand for performance.

Some will argue that what I have just described does not warrant the term "indulgence." Well, I had the other kind, too.

Shortly before I was born, Leah moved into our home. Leah was a childless widow who took up residence in our home as a live-in helper, since the constant flow of people who ate at our home was more than Mother could manage alone.

When I arrived, Leah virtually adopted me. My earliest memories are of her caring for me, preparing my meals, putting me to bed, and sitting on the bed, rocking it until I fell asleep. Leah had a repertoire of but a few bedtime stories, which she repeated a thousand times over. Thus, in addition to affectionate parents, there was a childless woman whose total preoccupation was to indulge my every whim. I thus cannot see indulgence *per se* as being incriminated as the cause for narcissism or sociopathy, both of which I am presumptuous enough to disown. The crucial point, I believe, is the overriding importance of being held to a code of behavior.

⸙

As a child, I was somewhat of a chess prodigy and was invariably triumphant when playing with the men in the synagogue after services. One Rosh Hoshanah, when I was nine, a rabbi from Chicago guested at our home, and in the afternoon when Father was resting, he asked if I wished to play chess. I was surprised at this, being under the impression that playing chess on Rosh Hoshanah was prohibited; but the rabbi's assurance that it was permissible was sufficient for me. He was a good player, but I eventually won.

That evening, the second night of Rosh Hoshanah, I was told that Father wished to see me in his study. When I came in, he was studying, and I remained silent. After a few moments, he looked up from his books. "You played chess on Rosh Hoshanah?" he asked quietly.

"Yes," I said, "Rabbi C. said it was permissible."

Father looked back down to his books, slowly shaking his head in the negative. The message was clear. Even though Rabbi C. was correct according to the letter of the law, it was not in the spirit of Rosh Hoshanah to play chess, and I knew better than that. (The admonition, "You *should have known* better," is an insult because it chastises one for his ignorance. "You *know* better than that" is merely stating an oversight and is not insulting.)

As I had not been dismissed, I remained standing in silence while Father continued his reading. The remorse during these few minutes was most profound. There had not been any beating nor even any shouting, yet I resolved right then and there that never again as long as I lived would I violate the spirit of *Yom Tov* even with something that was technically permissible.

After a few moments, Father looked up, and there was a twinge of a smile accompanying the twinkle in his eye. "But you did checkmate him, didn't you?"

This little scene could not have been orchestrated more perfectly. I had done something wrong, and I was held accountable for my behavior. I sincerely regretted my misdeed, and this wiped the slate clean. It was now time for some positive stroking.

It is clear to me that Father would not have risked embarassing me in having me admit that I had been beaten in chess. He asked the question because he knew the answer, and this meant that he had the confidence in me that I was a winner.

Did I analyze all this at the age of eight? Of course not. But although I did not understand the dynamics, the positive effect on my self-esteem was not diminished.

One can admonish and chastise without crushing another's ego. Sternness need not be cruel to be effective. Similarly, correcting another's mistake need not be done in a demeaning manner.

We had an instructor in yeshiva who would stimulate students to challenge him. He clearly relished their arguments, and when it was necessary to correct them, he would try to preserve their sense of triumph while pointing out a fallacy or oversight in their reasoning.

In his broken English he would say, "You right! You a hundred prozent right! Now I show you where you wrong."

This was not at all an internal contradiction. The student had presented a very cogent argument, and that needed to be acknowledged. The fact that the argument was not valid did not detract from his achievement.

Incidentally, this is a truism which I have used many times. You may be one hundred percent right, yet I can show you where you are wrong.

❧

All mothers like to boast about their children's wise sayings, and my mother was no exception. So I heard her tell many times how when I was a child and wanted ice cream, I was told that I could not have any because I was *fleishig* (had eaten meat) and was not permitted ice cream for a period of time. My response was "Just give me a glass of milk and you will see how fast I can become *milchig*."

I don't know whether I actually remember this incident or imagine I remember it. In any event, it is a vague memory at best, which means that it had to occur before I was five, because I remember most things that happened after five.

There is significance and value in teaching a four-year-old to postpone. There are things that are categorically forbidden, and although it requires teaching and training to achieve abstention, the task is not formidable. But what if the goal is not to convey that something is intrinsically wrong or evil, but that although it is in itself good, it must be delayed until an appropriate time. Where in children's experience are they taught postponement of gratification? And if there is no prototype for this in their upbringing, how can we suddenly spring such requirements on them as they grow older?

If there was ever a need to teach young children to postpone, it is in the era of the "now" generation, where everything is expected to happen within moments. And in our everday lives we cannot convert one status to another with the push of a button. The capacity to delay is one of the distinctive features of the human being. Animals are driven by impulse, and seek immediate gratification. The human being must have the self-mastery and control which enable him to postpone.

My childish suggestion of fifty years ago appears to be the accepted, mature practice in today's world. Something is restricted? We find a way to circumvent the restriction.

If you want your children to develop self-mastery not only in avoiding what is bad, but also in being able to delay or postpone, begin this training while they are tots. Let them know that even nourishing ice cream may have to be delayed if they are *fleishig*, and also that there is no magical way of becoming instantaneously *unfleishig*.

◆§ §◆

One thing which was not tolerated in our home was any kind of curse or malediction. Father used to interpret the Biblical prohibition, "*Elokim lo tkallel,*" (literally, do not curse God) to mean, "A Godly person does not curse."

It was a rare occasion to see Father really angry. However, if his threshold was finally exceeded and he did become angry, the worst invective he could hurl was "May he have soft, fresh bread and hard butter," a malediction which he had learned from his mother.

Anyone who has had the frustrating experience of trying to apply cold, hard butter to soft bread can well understand how intensely Father must have been provoked to wish this on someone. But he taught us that even anger does not have to be manifested destructively.

⁂

The proscription against cursing also emphasized the potency of words. The popular proverb "Sticks and stones can break my bones, but words will not hurt me," is wrong and misleading. Words *can* be destructive, and the tongue can be more malevolent than the sword.

Father's method of discouraging *lashon hara* (literally "evil talk" or gossip) would be to say, "Let's talk about more pleasant things." With many guests at the table, someone would invariably make some negative comments about someone else. To rebuke that person for talking *lashon hara* would have been humiliating. Instead, Father would steer the conversation toward a benign subject, often introduced with the above comment.

Father often told the story of the *Chafetz Chayim,* Rabbi Israel Meir HaCohen, the sage of the previous generation, who dedicated his life toward discouraging *lashon hara.*

The *Chafetz Chayim* was once en route home when travel conditions jeopardized his arrival before Friday evening, and he spent *Shabbos* at an inn. He shared the *Shabbos* table with other travelers, several of whom happened to be horse traders. The latter dominated the conversation at the *Shab-*

bos table with shop talk about horses: strong horses, weak horses, breeding horses, etc.

After *Shabbos*, someone informed the innkeeper that he had hosted the great *Chafetz Chayim* that *Shabbos*. The innkeeper came to the *Chafetz Chayim* and apologized profusely. "I did not accord you the proper respect that is your due," he said. "I had no idea who you were. I feel so badly having placed you at the table with those people who spoke of nothing but horses all *Shabbos*. I am sure you were offended by the mundane and vulgar character of the conversation, and I am terribly sorry for this."

The *Chafetz Chayim* smiled. "You have nothing to apologize for, my dear friend," he said. "You treated me admirably, and I lacked for nothing. As far as the conversation is concerned, I was not in the least offended. You see, my child, had they talked about people, I would have been exposed to hearing *lashon hara,* which is so grave a sin. But since they talked only about horses, why, there is nothing wrong with that."

The utmost respect for utterances was conveyed by yet another story which I heard Father tell many times, and the repetition indicated that he felt its message was important.

If I were ever challenged by anyone about any assertion, and tried to support my assertion by saying, "I swear that is true," or "So help me," or anything equivalent to an oath, I would receive a glance from Father which constituted a sharp rebuke. Taking an oath was not permitted, even if the fact were true.

Father told of Rabbi Chajkel, who shared the community leadership with Rabbi Azriel, the *dayan*. (Many communities had a *dayan,* or magistrate, whose function was to be the judge or arbitrator in various disputes or litigations.)

The two rabbis were close friends, and frequently studied Torah together.

One time Rabbi Azriel was in Rabbi Chajkel's study, when a woman came in and asked Rabbi Chajkel to hold 500 rubles for her in safekeeping. She was leaving town for a few days, and had no one else to whom she could entrust the money.

Later that day, Rabbi Chajkel tried to locate the money but could not find it. He searched all the drawers and cabinets in his study and went through the pockets of all his garments, but to no avail. The money was gone.

With a heavy heart, Rabbi Chajkel went to Rabbi Azriel's home. He asked him whether he had perhaps noticed what he had done with the money which the woman gave him. Rabbi Azriel said that he had not seen him do anything with the money, and that to the best of his recollection, it had remained on the desk.

Rabbi Chajkel sighed deeply, "The money is gone, Reb Azriel," he said. "I have searched everywhere. You and I were the only two people present. I know this sounds absurd, Reb Azriel, but this money was entrusted to me, and although you are beyond suspicion, I am obligated by *halacha* to request that you take an oath that you did not take it."

Rabbi Azriel was shaken. "Take an oath, Reb Chajkel?" he asked. "I should swear? Can you give me just a bit of time to give this some thought?"

"Of course," Rabbi Chajkel answered and left Rabbi Azriel's study.

That evening Rabbi Azriel came to Rabbi Chajkel. "Here are 275 rubles," he said. "That is all I have."

Rabbi Chajkel was upset. He knew that Rabbi Azriel's

earnings were very meager, and that he did not own 275 rubles. What was the meaning of this? He knew that Rabbi Azriel was under great pressure to provide a dowry for his daughter who was soon to marry. Could it be that Rabbi Azriel had been unable to resist the temptation, and that confronted with the possible cancellation of the wedding if he failed to provide a dowry, Rabbi Azriel had weakened and had taken the money? That was absurd! But how else would he explain Rabbi Azriel's having a sum so large as 275 rubles?

"I cannot compromise," Rabbi Chajkel said. "If I do not have the 500 rubles to return to the woman, I must demand that you swear."

"Give me one more day," Rabbi Azriel pleaded.

The following day, Rabbi Azriel returned and gave Rabbi Chajkel an additional 125 rubles. "This is all I have," he said.

Rabbi Chajkel was stern. He was now convinced that Rabbi Azriel had succumbed to the stress of his daughter's wedding needs and had indeed taken the money. Not, God forbid, with an intent to steal, but just to borrow it for a few weeks until after the wedding, when he would somehow repay it. For how else would the impoverished Rabbi Azriel have gotten 400 rubles in two days?

"500 rubles, Reb Azriel," said Rabbi Chajkel. "Not one kopek less."

"Here is a promissory note to the woman for 100 rubles," said Rabbi Azriel. "I will pay it within 30 days. More I cannot do."

"Good enough," said Rabbi Chajkel. "I shall prevail upon the woman to accept your note."

The next few days, when Rabbi Chajkel met Rabbi Azriel, he looked away. If he saw him coming from afar, he tried to avoid meeting him. He could not make peace with the thought that his trusted *chaver* (close friend) had yielded to temptation and had taken something belonging to another.

Friday afternoon, Rabbi Chajkel was preparing his study for *Shabbos*. The *Mizrach* plaque (a decorative plaque designating which direction was east, so that anyone praying in that room would know which direction to face toward Jerusalem) was hanging crooked, and as he lifted it to hang it straight, the bundle of 500 rubles fell out! Rabbi Chajkel suddenly recalled that he had hidden the money there. He emitted a loud shriek and fell to the ground in a faint.

Rabbi Chajkel's family, hearing the loud cry, came running and revived him. As he came to, he tore at his beard and wept uncontrollably. "What have I done!" he cried. "I falsely accused a *zaddik* of a terrible crime! How could I ever have done such a thing! I have sinned against an innocent man and against God!" Nothing his family could say would console him.

In the midst of his weeping and self-flagellation, Rabbi Chajkel said, "I must go to the *zaddik*, Reb Azriel. I must ask his forgiveness. He may spit at me and throw me out of his house, the rotten cur that I am! How I have caused him to suffer needlessly!"

Rabbi Chajkel ran to Rabbi Azriel's home. Breathelessly he threw open the door. "Reb Azriel, forgive me!" he cried. "I know I am unworthy of your forgiveness, but as a God-fearing person, I ask you to do as Almighty God does, and forgive the most despicable sinners when they repent their sins!"

Rabbi Azriel's wife came in. "Reb Chajkel," she said, "why do you shout? Reb Azriel is not in the house. He has left to *shul* already."

Rabbi Chajkel ran out and hurried to the *shul.* A small crowd had already gathered for *Mincha.* He ran to the pulpit and pounded on the pulpit for attention.

"Hear me, good people," he cried. "Hear me, Reb Azriel the *zaddik.* For 20 years, I have been your Rabbi, but I do not deserve to be your Rabbi. I have sinned against an innocent man. I have falsely accused a *zaddik* of a grave crime. I am not worthy for the earth to support me." The tears flowed freely down his cheeks. He turned and ran to the *aron hakodesh* (the ark containing the Torah), threw open its doors, and shouted, "Only you, God, can forgive me!"

Rabbi Azriel came up and put his arm around his *chaver.* "Calm down, Reb Chajkel," he pleaded. "Please, calm yourself. I would gladly forgive you wholeheartedly if there was something which required forgiveness. But what is there to forgive, Reb Chajkel? You have done nothing wrong."

"Nothing wrong?" asked Rabbi Chajkel. "Nothing wrong to accuse my bosom friend, a true *zaddik,* of so menial an act? You mock at me, Reb Azriel. Yes, you mock at me. But I deserve it, and much more. Whatever you wish to do to me, Reb Azriel, I accept, to my great shame."

"Heaven forbid that I mock at you, Reb Chajkel," said Rabbi Azriel. "You had no other course. There was no one else in the room but you and me, and when you could not locate the money, you had no choice but to conclude that I took it, and to demand that I swear my innocence.

"When I heard that I must swear," Rabbi Azriel continued, "I shuddered. Never in my life have I taken an oath. I therefore took the 250 rubles that I had borrowed for my daughter's wedding, and sold my wife's jewelry for another 25 rubles.

"When you told me that this was not enough," Rabbi

Azriel continued, "I sold my library for 125 rubles. I am so grateful, Reb Chajkel, that you took the promissory note for 100 rubles. I am so grateful, for otherwise I do not know what I would have done. I would have been compelled to swear. To swear, even when you know you are swearing the truth, is awesome. You spared me, Reb Chajkel, by accepting my note. I shall never forget this kindness."

Father had made his point. One's mouth is not a grinder, to spew out indiscriminately. The tongue is a powerful instrument. It can be a constructive tool or a destructive weapon. Three times each day, we conclude the *amidah* with the prayer, "My God, guard my tongue from evil, and my lips from speaking falsehood." Father taught us to respect our gift of speech.

⁂

Father could take anything with equanimity. Anything, that is, except illness among his children. When we grew up and left home, we had to be extremely cautious not to let on when any of us, whether children or grandchildren, had even anything as minor as the sniffles.

When I was Father's assistant rabbi and lived nearby, it was difficult to keep him from finding out when one of our children was sick. I knew what to expect. Early in the morning, I would find Father standing at our front door, looking through the window, trying to detect whether anyone was awake so that he could find out how the child was feeling. He did not dare call nor ring the bell, lest he awaken any of us, but he stood at the door for hours, hoping to see someone moving about inside.

One time Father underwent surgery, and he developed a severe post-operative hemorrhage which necessitated multiple blood transfusions. Inasmuch as I was living a long distance away at the time, I tried to stay in contact with his physician or with the special nurse who attended him.

The very day he received the transfusions, I called his hospital room, expecting to talk to the nurse. To my surprise, Father answered the phone. "How are you feeling?" I asked. "And how come you are answering the phone in your condition?"

"You sound hoarse to me," Father responded. "Are you sure you don't have a cold?"

That was what the man was like. While he was in a most precarious condition himself, his concern was not about his hemorrhage, but whether I had the sniffles.

❧

Reb Ber of Rodscitz had occasion to lodge overnight at an inn. The following morning he asked the innkeeper, "Where did you get that enchanted chime clock? Each time the clock chimed the hour, I felt a surge of elation, until finally I could not restrain myself and had to get out of bed and dance for joy."

The innkeeper responded, "This clock belonged to a traveler who did not have the money to pay for his lodging. He left the clock as a pledge, and said he would stop by and redeem it on his way back."

"Do you know whether the man was perhaps of the family of the Rebbe of Lublin?" Reb Ber asked. "This marvelous clock could only have belonged to the Rebbe of Lublin."

"That I cannot tell you for certain," the innkeeper said.

"But now that you mention it, I think I did hear the traveler refer to his grandfather as the Rebbe of Lubin."

"I knew this must be so," Reb Ber said. "You see, a clock is generally a depressing instrument. It is constantly telling you that moments of your life have passed by and are irretrievable. Each time a clock chimes you are thus made aware that another segment of your life is gone forever, and that is a depressing thought.

"Not so with the clock of the Rebbe of Lublin. Each time his clock chimed, it indicated that we are so much closer to the redemption of *Moshiach* (Messiah). This is a clock that heralds good tidings. It is an elating timepiece rather than a depressing one."

I think that one of the reasons we celebrate birthdays is to attempt to overcome the otherwise depressive nature of the day that would result from the awareness that another year of our lives has passed into history, and too often we are neither wealthier nor wiser than we were a year earlier. We have come just a bit closer to the ultimate end of our lives. This is too depressing a feeling, and we escape this by celebrating, which is a rather good defense.

If, however, life is perceived as a process toward a goal, then the passing of time need not be at all depressing. Quite the contrary, if one is on a long journey, one feels happier as one gets closer to the destination.

Jewishness teaches, "This world is but an antechamber to the palace. Prepare yourself in the antechamber so that you may enter the palace." (Ethics of the Fathers 4:16). One need only not while away the time idly.

Whether one understands the passage of time as coming closer to one's personal salvation, or as with the Rebbe of

Lublin, the salvation of mankind, it is a philosophy that can increase the joy in life.

ᘛ§ ᘚ

During the Yom Kippur services, a man was absorbed in reciting the literature. He was swaying to and fro, with the *talis* covering his head, and singing the prayers with a solemn, nay mournful melody.

Another worshipper approached him. "What is it about these prayers that makes you cry?" he asked.

"Why, don't you see?" the man responded. "The whole tragedy of human life is described here. As it says, 'What is man? His origin is dust, and he returns to dust.' "

"You call that a tragedy?" the other man responded. "If it had said that man was made out of gold and turns into dust, *that* would indeed be a tragedy. But if his origin is dust and he returns to dust, and in the interim he has the opportunity to make a *L'chayim* (the usual greeting at a toast), why, that is not a tragedy. I see that as pure profit!"

It is all in the way you look at it. *Lebedig, kinderlach, lebedig*!

ᘛ§ ᘚ

A chassid whose business involved purchasing forests for lumber once suffered a major economic loss when the price of lumber fell precipitously. He came to his Rebbe and complained about his misfortune.

The Rebbe empathized with him, then said:

"Many things happen which we perceive to be misfortunes, only to discover at a later date that the outcome was favorable. If we allow ourselves to anguish over them, then we cause the Almighty to suffer along with us, for the Psalmist says, 'I am with him in his distress.' (Psalms 91: 15) Now tell me, my child, is it really worth it, because of a few pieces of wood, to put the Almighty in anguish?"

When the self is the sole measure of all things, anything which causes distress to the self is perceived as a great evil. When the self is seen as but a small part of a greater whole, the impact of a blow is diffused, and the pain is far less severe.

I regret that I came to learn this so late in life. I am certain that many times I was upset by various things which were really relatively trivial, and did not warrant aggravation. I am equally certain that my parents, aware of my being upset, were in turn distressed by this. That I allowed myself to be hurt by things which later proved to be of no consequence is merely my own folly, but that I thereby caused my parents unnecessary misery is a heavy burden.

The fact that one person's distress can affect another is said to be one of the reasons why sharing your troubles with another person can ameliorate suffering. Suppose that for whatever reason, it was decreed by the heavenly tribunal that person "A" undergo a painful experience. A unburdens himself to his friend "B". If B, as a true friend, is distressed by what is happening to A, then A must be relieved of his misery, because it is now causing B distress, and B was *not* decreed to suffer.

To genuinely feel the hurt of another person is therefore to help him, even if you can do nothing active to change his situation.

In a culture so obsessed with love and in which young people marry because they have "fallen in love," there must be something drastically wrong when better than forty per cent of all marriages terminate in divorce, some so quickly that one wonders whether the partners even had the opportunity to discover whether or not they were indeed in love.

It would seem that if the people involved had indeed "fallen in love," such love should have had greater substance and durability.

If we just note what usage is given to the word "love," the mystery is solved. One can just "love" a fashionable garment, and a tasty dish can be "loved".

It is abundantly clear that the word "love" is generally used to refer to gratification of one's desires. I "love" something that gives me a pleasant sensation. In this sense, love is essentially self-love, and the so-called love of another simply means that the other person satisfies *my* desires.

It is little wonder, then, that relationships based on love which is self-directed can be very fleeting. When the person no longer adequately satisfies my desires, or when the person constitutes a burden in such a way that the demands upon me outweigh the gratification, or if I find another person who can provide me with greater gratification, then the basis for the relationship ceases and the relationship terminates.

Not all love, however, must be self-love. There does exist an outwardly-directed love, which emanates from the appreciation and admiration of another person. Outwardly-directed love has totally different characteristics than self-directed love.

Love that is not self-directed is unfortunately so rare that it may be difficult for us to comprehend it. As an example, take the Biblical account of Jacob's love for Rachel: "Jacob worked for seven years to win the hand of Rachel, but it appeared to him as only several days because of his great love for her." (Genesis XXIX: 18-20).

At first glance, this makes no sense. For the man who is separated from the woman he loves, every day seems like an eternity. Why then does the Torah state that in Jacob's profound love for Rachel, seven years appeared to him as only several days?

We do not understand this because the love we are so familiar with is primarily self-directed, and when desires are denied, even a brief period of frustration may appear endless. Outwardly-directed love obeys different rules. Long periods may appear brief; and if we cannot understand this, it is probably because we simply have no concept of what outwardly-directed love is.

I believe that I had the opportunity to witness an outwardly-directed love relationship in my parents. Firstly, they were not drawn together by infatuation or by a desire for the other to satisfy the self. Their marriage was totally arranged by their parents. They met for the first time under the *chupah* (the ritual marriage canopy). Secondly, they knew that they were to share their lives in order to achieve a goal in which they both believed, to have a family and to transmit to their children the heritage which they had received.

Mother and Father soon grew to appreciate one another. In the early days of their marriage they were subjected to stresses and divisive forces which would certainly have shattered any relationship based on self-gratification. They remained together because the bond was such that it could not be overcome by frustration and distress.

Outwardly-directed love is characterized not by what the other partner can provide for me, but by what I can do for him or her.

Fifty-two years later, Father suffered his terminal illness. He knew he had cancer of the pancreas, but the thought of death did not frighten him. Quite the contrary, he had been anticipating something of the sort. A few weeks before his first symptoms had occurred, Grandfather had appeared to him in a dream and had said, "You have nothing to fear. It is just like walking out of one room and into another." The only serious concern that Father had was that a long and debilitating illness would be a burden on the family.

Father was extremely well-versed medically. His frequent conferences with physicians and his daily visits to the hospital had kept him informed of the most recent medical advances. When the doctor suggested chemotherapy, Father said, "You know as well as I do that chemotherapy for cancer of the pancreas is not effective. All it can do is produce undesirable side-effects. If it could prolong life, then I would probably be required by *halacha* to do everything humanly possible to live longer, even if it meant living with distress. However, there is certainly no requirement to subject one's self to a treatment which will cause a great deal of misery and not prolong life." The doctor had to agree that Father was right.

In his conversation with Mother, however, the doctor indicated that chemotherapy might prolong life by perhaps three months. Mother was adamant. As long as there was anything that could be done, it must be done. Who knows but that during those three months, the long awaited breakthrough in a cancer cure might come about.

"Foolishness," said Father. But Mother would not yield.

One time Father and I were alone, and he said, "You know, to subject myself to the misery of chemotherapy when there is nothing to be gained is ridiculous. But if it is not done, Mother will not be at ease. During our marriage I have done many things for Mother's happiness; and if I have the opportunity to do one last thing for her, I will not turn it down."

Our language lacks a word to distinguish one type of love from another. The same word that is used to express how one feels about meat and potatoes is also used to describe a devotion of self-sacrifice. Perhaps even our ideas become as impoverished as our words. How tragic.

◆§ §◆

Father often told the story of a young child who was learning to read Hebrew. The teacher told him that two "yuds" together, (״) are a representation of the name of God and should be read as such.

Whenever the child came to the end of a sentence in *chumash*, he pronounced the name of God. When asked why, he said that at the end of each sentence there were two "yuds," (the two dots : signifying the end of a sentence).

"No, no" said the teacher. "When you see two "yuds" standing side by side, that refers to God. If one is standing above the other, that is the end of a phrase."

Father would say,"The Divine presence is only where two Jews (two "yuds") stand alongside one another, relating as equals. If one "yud" considers himself to be above and superior to another, there is no Divine presence. Quite the contrary, that indicates a termination."

◆§ §◆

Every Friday night at the *Shabbos* dinner, Father would expound on the Torah, usually on the portion of that week. From the little that I remember, it is painfully evident how much I have not retained. Most of what I recall is clearly from what I heard in my childhood years. Of course, I did not understand much of it at the time I heard it, but that is the way with learning. Like a planted seed, it bears fruit much later.

I recall Father commenting on Moses' vision of the burning thornbush. Moses observed the thornbush aflame, yet not being consumed. "I must go and see," said Moses, "why the thornbush burns yet is not consumed." Then God revealed Himself to Moses, saying, "I am the God of thy forefathers, Abraham, Isaac, and Jacob." (Exodus III: 3, 6)

"Throughout history," Father said, "we have repeatedly observed the phenomenon of Jews who were otherwise distant from Jewishness, who did not clearly identify themselves as Jews, and who strayed from Jewish practices. Yet, when various oppressors demanded that they renounce their faith or forfeit their lives, many chose *kiddush Hashem,* sacrificing their lives rather than deny their Jewishness. Rabbi Jacob of Emden reported that during the Inquisition, many sophisticated Jews yielded to conversion, whereas many simple and unpretentious folk went to the stake, with *Shema Yisroel* on their lips.

"This is the wondrous vision which Moses beheld," Father said. "The thornbush represents the Jew who appears to be completely unproductive: dry, empty of fruit, providing no shade, barren of all Jewishness. Yet when put to the supreme test, he comes alive with a burning fervor which gives a glow extending through time and space. 'How wondrous' said Moses. 'Whence comes so intense a rapture in someone who is not otherwise saturated with Jewishness?'

"The Divine answer was, 'This is the heritage of the forefathers Abraham, Isaac, and Jacob. Within every Jew there is a nucleus of Jewishness, a spark of the *neshama* that was implanted by the Patriarchs and which is the heritage of all their descendants. At any moment, that concealed spark can burst into an intense and absolute devotion. No Jew dare ever be written off as lost to his people.' "

Of course, performance of the *mitzvohs* can cause the spark to burst into flame. Father used to tell of a Jew in Kiev who had totally assimilated, and had become the head of a bank, something totally unattainable in czarist Russia for anyone even remotely suspected of being Jewish.

Once, while on vacation at a seashore, this man happened to be at the scene where a body was washed ashore. There was no way of identifying the drowned man, but because he was wearing *tzizis* (a small *talis* worn as an undergarment), he was recognized as being Jewish and was given a Jewish burial.

The assimilated banker reasoned that although he had renounced all Jewish identity in order to achieve his social and economic status, this was relevant only in this world, but that after his death, when his true identity would no longer be a hindrance, he wished to be buried as a Jew. He therefore began wearing the *tzizis* undergarment.

The banker slowly began a metamorphosis, with progressive adoption of Jewish practices. He had to resign his position at the bank, and eventually became a prominent member of the Jewish community.

"Never despair of a Jewish *neshama*," Father used to say.

Similarly, Father used to comment on the opinion of Rashi

(Genesis VII: 7) that Noah did not enter the ark until the rising water forced him to do so, because he did not believe in the coming of the deluge, although God had predicted it.

"How can it be," Father asked, "that as great a *zaddik* as Noah doubted the word of God?

"The answer is," Father said, "that Noah's belief in the inherent goodness of man was so great, that he was convinced that mankind would yet repent and forestall the Divine wrath." The essential goodness of man was a recurrent theme of Father's.

Many years later, my psychiatric practice led me in the direction of rehabilitating persons who had fallen victim to alcoholism and drug addiction. Thank God, this effort has been very rewarding, as I have been privileged to witness thousands of virtually miraculous successes in treatment.

I am often asked how one can have the patience to persist in pursuing recovery for a person who has had repeated relapses and whose persistent failure to recover must surely be frustrating to the point of utter despair.

The answer is that the word "despair" was rendered alien to my vocabulary. Despair is the absolute abandonment of hope, and Father taught that the Divine spark is in every human; whereas its glow may be diminished almost to the point of extinction, it is never completely extinguished.

⁂

I remember Father often repeating the story of the Rebbe of Pscizche who once encountered his future disciple, who was later to become the Rebbe of Kotzk.

"Young man," the Rebbe of Pscizche demanded, "Where

can one find God?"

"Everywhere!" the young man responded. "His glory fills the universe."

"Young man," the Pscizcher repeated. "I asked you, where can one find God?"

"There is no place in the universe that is void of His presence," the Kotzker answered.

"Young man, haven't you heard me?" the Pscizcher asked. "Tell me, where can one find God?"

The Kotzker was stymied. "Well, if I don't know, then please tell me," he said.

The Pscizcher then said, "Listen to me, young man. God can only be found where He is welcomed and permitted entrance."

What was the point in Father's repeating this story so often? I think he wanted to impress us that we must not take God for granted. In our profession of belief in the omnipresence of God, it is easy to lose sight of the fact that God may choose to shun a hostile environment. If we wish to be in the presence of God, we must earn it.

⁂

Great-grandfather, the first Rebbe of Bobov, was once sitting with a group of his chassidim, and their discussion culminated in the discovery that this particular day was a special occasion that deserved to be celebrated with a *L'chayim.* One of the group offered to pay for the refreshments, but no one volunteered to go make the purchase. Great-grandfather then said, "Just hand me the money. I have a young boy who will be glad to go."

After a rather extended lapse of time, Great-grandfather

returned with the refreshments, and it became obvious to the very embarrassed chassidim that the Rebbe himself must have performed the errand.

Noticing their discomfort, Great-grandfather said, "I did not mislead you at all. You see, many people outgrow their youth and become old men. I have never let the spirit of my youth depart. As I grew older, I always took along with me the 'young boy' that I had been. It was that 'young boy' in me that did the errand."

Youth has great capacity for learning, retaining, innovating, and creating. The psychic energies of youth are enormous. As we mellow, we tend to allow these energies to wane, and the growth capacities to atrophy. We think of this as the natural and inevitable course of maturation.

Not so, said Great-grandfather. If our energies and growth capacities weaken, it is because we have allowed them to do so. It is due more to laziness than to an inexorable process of aging that we plateau and then deteriorate. We become complacent, self-satisifed, too tolerant of the goals we have achieved. To be forever striving for knowledge, for new insights, for fresh perspectives, that is the way we can take youth along far into our biologic old age.

Just note the difference between young children, whom you cannot get to go to bed, and older people, who look forward to sleep. The child is curious about his world, and can always think of thousands of things to do. This spirit of inquisitiveness and creativity keeps him invigorated. For the young child, there are just not enough hours in the day. The older person who loses this initiative and is essentially content with the *status quo* becomes fatigued, not so much because of a worn-out or spent physiologic system, but because of lack of stimulation.

The sages said it succinctly. "Torah must be totally new to you each day " (Rashi, Deut. XXVI:16). At eighty-five as at five, the challenge of learning and achieving must be exciting and stimulating. "They will yet blossom in their old age," says the psalmist (Psalms 92:15). This is the true fountain of youth.

◆

People would consult Father with various problems, some so severe that there seemed to be no solution. Father would reassure them that even when human ingenuity appeared to be incapable of resolving a problem, God worked in wondrous ways. Only faith and trust in God were necessary.

Occasionally, Father would tell people in despair about an incident with the Rebbe of Apt. One of the citizens of Apt was a very wealthy man, who owned several factories and had wide real estate holdings. His children, all of whom were grown, had all become independently wealthy. He was the most influential and highly respected citizen of the community.

One day, he told the Rebbe that he was much bothered by the verse in the daily prayers which reads, "God lowers the mighty to the ground, and lifts the down-trodden to the heights of heaven."

"In what manner could God humble me?" he asked. "If some of my businesses were to fail, then the others would still survive. Certainly God would not ruin the economy of an entire nation just to get at me. And if in some way I were to lose all my assets, then my children are independently wealthy. And even if something were to happen to my children, I am certain that the community would not forget my years of devotion and support. How would God single me out to lower me to the ground?"

The Rebbe rebuked him sharply. "Do not be so foolish as

to challenge God. Simply accept on faith that nothing is beyond Him."

Several days later, the man returned. "I am obsessed with this conflict," he said. "I simply cannot conceive how God could single me out for ruin without causing a major calamity." Again the Rebbe sent him away with a rebuke. When the man persisted day after day, the Rebbe finally said, "The Almighty can do anything."

Later that day, the wealthy man began to be annoyed by the thought that he should convert to another religion. At first, he was able to dismiss the thought as an absurdity, but it gradually increased in intensity and he could not dismiss it from his mind. Soon he was totally consumed by an irresistable urge, and, as one possessed, found himself in the priest's rectory, professing his desire to convert.

The priest was skeptical. "Did you come to mock me?" he asked. "I know who you are. You are the most prominent member of the Jewish community. I cannot believe you are sincere in your claim of wishing to convert. This is some sort of jest for which I have little patience."

Still seized by this strange, passionate desire, the man fell to his knees and began crying, pleading with the priest to believe him and accept him.

The priest, noting his tears and persistence finally said, "I still have difficulty in accepting your sincerity. However, if you genuinely wish to convert, you must demonstrate this by transferring title of everything you own to the church. If you do this, then and only then will I believe you are sincere."

Unable to resist the intense urge which had overtaken him, the man wrote out a document giving everything he owned to the church. The priest put the document into his desk, and told the man to wait a bit, for he would return shortly for the conversion ritual.

No sooner had the priest left, that the strange urge abruptly disappeared. As if awakening from a nightmare, the man looked about him. "What on earth am I doing inside a church?" he said, and promptly ran out.

The man then remembered what had transpired. He realized that he was now personally impoverished. He owned nothing. He did not dare contact his family. What would they say of him when they found out he was a *meshumed* (defector from Judaism)? And the community? All the years of his service would be nothing in the face of what he had just done! He walked the streets, bewildered, not knowing where to turn. He was now poor and terribly alone.

It was late at night when it occurred to him that the Rebbe might have compassion, for the Rebbe never turned anyone away. He came into the Rebbe's study, broke into profuse tears, and confessed to the Rebbe what he had done.

The Rebbe comforted him. "Now, my child," he said. "Do you see how simple it is for God to humble someone?"

The man continued weeping. "I was foolish to doubt the powers of God. I should have listened to your chastisement. But now I am doomed forever. Nothing can save me."

"But you forget the second half of the prayer," the Rebbe said. "'He elevates the downtrodden to the heights of heaven.' You must now have faith that God can do this too. Go home and sleep, and trust in the salvation of God."

The following morning, there was talk in the streets of a flash fire that had occurred in the church, destroying part of the rectory. There was no desk, no document, no evidence that anything had happened.

Father would tell this story to those who needed to hear that when human ingenuity has been exhausted, when there seems to be no escape from a dilemma, one must never lose faith in the infinite wisdom and power of God.

◆§ §◆

If we set unreasonably high goals for our children, do we cause them to give up trying because our expectations are beyond reality?

Too often our perception of "reality" is incorrect. Who knows what undeveloped strengths and potential may lie dormant in a child? Psychologists tell us that most people use only a small fraction of their brain capacity. With the appropriate stimulation, and with the love, security, and confidence that parents can provide, children might well cultivate talents and skills which may have gone unnoticed by their parents.

I remember that as small children, when we lit the Chanuka candles, Mother would tell us that when she was a child of five, she stood near her grandfather, the first Rebbe of Bobov, when he kindled the Chanuka menorah. Great-grandfather would sit in front of the glowing wicks, immersed in profound meditation.

Mother related that she asked him, "Zeide, what are you thinking of now?"

Great-grandfather turned to the child and said, "I am praying that you have good children."

A few moments later Mother again interrupted the meditation. "Zeide," she asked, "what are you thinking of *now*?"

This time the response was, "I am praying that *your* children have good children."

At the age of five, Mother was commissioned with a task. Great-grandfather died soon afterward, but had charged the child with a duty. Mother's recollection of this incident obviously indicated that this memory had never left her.

I was not much older than five when Mother conveyed this memory and message to me, and I transmitted it to my children when they were of that age.

Our sages tell us that prayer alone can only accomplish half the task, and that man's effort must complete the remainder. But the Zeide's prayer was more than a supplication to God. It was also a message to Mother, then a child of five, that there were expectations of her.

Do not hesitate to expect accomplishments of your children. Pray to God for His blessings, give your children the nurturing, love, and security essential for optimum growth, and above all, have confidence and trust in their capacities to achieve.

❧

In many Jewish homes, it is customary to serve *farfel tzimmis* (a side dish of toasted egg barley) as part of the *Shabbos* eve dinner menu.

It is said that this tradition began with the Baal Shem Tov, who exploited a play on words for a symbolic teaching.

The word "*farfallen*" in Yiddish means "bygone" or "over and done with." The Baal Shem Tov taught that when one realizes the mistakes or wrongdoings that one has committed, sincerely regrets them, and makes a sincere resolution never to repeat the same act again, that is the essence and totality of repentance. Ruminating on mistakes of the past is not only futile, but destructive. It depresses a person and drains off energy which could be used constructively.

Friday night marks the end of the work week, and *Shabbos* provides an opportunity for study, prayer, and meditation, and thinking about spiritual growth. Essential to this growth process is a release from the albatross of the past. *Shabbos* is thus the time for *tshuva* (returning) to the correct path in life. Mother reminded us of this every Friday night as she served the *farfel tzimmis.* "Remember, whatever was until today is *farfallen.*"

Having rid ourselves of the burdens of the past, we can truly rejoice in the joy of *Shabbos.* "People that sanctify the *Shabbos* will be satisfied and will take pleasure in Thy dominion." *Lebedig, kinderlach, lebedig.*

IV

On Spirituality

As a child, I knew some spiritual people.

What is a spiritual person? What is spirituality?

There are undoubtedly many complex definitions of spirituality, but for me, a very simple definition suffices. Spirituality is that which distinguishes man from lower forms of life.

Spirituality is not a scientific concept, and has nothing to do with intellect nor with the so-called "higher" mental functions. From the scientific viewpoint, man is *Homo sapiens*, or a gorilla with intellect. The distinctive feature of man is thus his intellect. If a sub-human form of life could somehow be made more intelligent, it would no longer be sub-human, but rather human. This kind of thinking has resulted in advocacy of infanticide for children who are mentally defective.

Lower forms of life are characterized by two instinctual drives: self-preservation and self-gratification. For them, there is nothing that transcends these self-directed drives. The human being who considers himself superior to say, a cow, because he can operate a computer and enjoy a television drama is in a sense actually superior only quantitatively, but has not risen above animalistic drives.

It might appear that altruistic and philanthropic deeds are qualitatively different and truly human, since they are directed toward someone other than oneself. However, just a bit of analysis will reveal that noble as these deeds may be, unless performed in compliance with the dictates of a Supreme Being, they emanate from internal drives, the frustration of which would result in feelings of distress; I am charitable because it hurts *me* to see someone in hunger or out in the cold. Hence, these outwardly-directed acts are ultimately self-gratifying. It is only when one acts at the behest of a supra-human being that one transcends the animal self and becmes uniquely human.

"And He blew into his nostrils a soul of living spirit," (Genesis II:7). This is how the creation of man is described: a soul derived from the very breath of God, and therefore Godly in nature; a living spirit totally distinct from the vital nature of animals. Man is a being that is capable of rising above himself, not only above his base nature, but even above his noble nature.

Spirituality gives man's being a purpose. Man is not a biological accident limited to self-gratification, but a being with a mission, one whose existence is goal-directed. The distinctive feature of humanity is thus spirituality rather than intellect.

The acid test of spirituality is man's response to suffering. Obviously, self-gratification and suffering are antithetical, since gratification requires the elimination of suffering. The stoic may adapt himself to accept suffering without external manifestation of distress and perhaps even with equanimity.

Only the person who lives a life which transcends his own being, and who rejoices in the knowledge that he is fulfilling the *purpose* of his creation, only that person can rejoice amidst his suffering.

Chassidic writings abound with the emphasis on joy. The Baal Shem Tov expounded his teachings of joy to Jews living under conditions of extreme poverty and severe oppression. The Baal Shem taught that the awareness that one has within himself a *neshama,* a Divine soul which is part of the Almighty, and that one has a unique and specific mission on earth, should so overshadow any suffering, that one should always be in a state of ecstasy. Indeed, said the Baal Shem, a lack of joy betrays a lack of true faith and conviction. *Lebedig, kinderlach, lebedig!*

Whereas scholars, people learned in both the revealed and esoteric Torah teachings, may have a deeper understanding of Godliness and *kedusha,* the fundamental belief in the Divine origin of one's soul and purposefulness in creation is accessible to everyone. Hence, the chassidic exaltation of every individual, the unlearned as well as the learned.

Reuben was a spiritual man. I never saw him unhappy. Every Tuesday night, I went to his home where he thoroughly enjoyed serving me *latkes* (potato pancakes), the likes of which have never been duplicated. On *Shabbos* morning, I would go to *shul* two hours before services to sit with Reuben while he recited *T'hillim* (Psalms). Even today, many decades later, I can vividly recall Reuben's melody.

Reuben was not a learned man. He would sit at the

Mishna classes given by my father, but I don't know how much he understood. He once told me that he had been orphaned as a child, and that no one had provided for his education, so that he only knew how to read, plus a few words of Hebrew that had become part of the vernacular. But Reuben was always manifestly happy.

Reuben had emigrated to America in the early 1900's. He peddled rags in his pushcart to provide for what had been a large family.

In Reuben's home I saw a family picture: Reuben, his wife, and eight sons and daughters. All but two children has predeceased him. Reuben was totally blind in one eye, and wore a thick lens over the other. He told me that he had become blind as a result of profuse weeping over the deaths of his young wife and six of their children. Whether or not this can be explained ophthalmologically, I believed him.

Although the weeping had ended, the suffering continued. Yet, the suffering was not an obstacle to joy.

For those whose lives are governed by the strivings for self-gratification, whether more sophisticated or less sophisticated, Reuben's experiences from childhood on and throughout his lifetime could have resulted in profound depression and perhaps even suicidal rejection of a cruel and hostile world.

But there was no bitterness in Reuben. I know. You see, a child can taste *all* the ingredients in *latkes,* and they were not in the least bitter. They were sweetened by the melody of *T'hillim:* "I have become weary with groaning; each night I soak my bed with tears" (Psalms VI: 7). "But I trust in Thy mercy, my heart is glad in Thy salvation." (Psalms XIII: 6).

Reuben was a spritual man.

⁂

Hershel was a *cohane* (of the priestly tribe) from whom I was privileged, as a child, to receive the priestly blessing on the holidays.

Hershel was an unlearned man. As a child, he had gone to *cheder* (Hebrew school) in Europe, and had learned to read Hebrew, but little beyond that. He came to America with the early Eastern European immigration, and peddled rags with his pushcart. He eventually worked his way up to a horse and wagon, and collected scrap metal, rags, and paper.

Before Sukkos (Feast of Tabernacles), Hershel would go out to the outskirts of the city with his horse and wagon to cut greenery to cover the *sukka.* This was the highlight of the year for me, because I could ride alongside him, and he even let me hold the reins.

Hershel eked out a meager but honest living. On *Shabbos* morning, he would come early to *shul* to recite the Psalms before the services. His only complaint was that he had to feed his horse on *Shabbos* before coming to *shul.* "What can I do?" he would say. "The Law says that you cannot let your animal go hungry."

Hershel was well liked. As a *cohane,* he would be called to officiate at the *pidyon haben* (redemption of the first-born) where he would receive the five silver dollars that the father is required to give to the *cohane.*

When Hershel took sick, he called his son and told him, "As soon as I go, open the drawer of the bureau. You will find a little cloth sack. Open it and follow instructions."

Immediately after Hershel breathed his last, the son obeyed his request. The little sack contained silver dollars and a gold piece. There was an accompanying note that read as follows:

"All my life I tried to earn an honest living. I never

knowingly cheated anyone. But who can say that he never, even accidentally, overcharged or short-changed anyone?

"I have pitiably little in *mitzvohs* (good deeds) to accompany me when I stand before the great Judge to give an account of my life. At least, I want to be dressed nicely. Sometimes nice clothes make a favorable impression.

"The only truly honest money that I can swear is justly mine are the coins in this sack. These are what I have received at the *pidyon haben* as the redemption gift. I know they are mine because the Torah assigned them to me as a *cohane*, regardless of whether I deserved them. My father was a *cohane*, and so am I. Therefore, this money is honestly mine.

"I want this money to be used to pay for my shrouds and all burial needs. This way if I appear nicely dressed and neatly groomed with honestly acquired fittings, the great Judge may be merciful in His judgment of me."

I have little doubt that Hershel's entrance into the heavenly court must have created quite a stir, for when else had the heavenly host ever seen so handsomely attired a person, wrapped with the glow of so many *mitzvohs*?

It is comforting to recall that the gold piece which was found in the sack was the one that I had given Hershel at the *pidyon haben* of my son.

Perhaps sophistication and sincerity are not mutually exclusive, yet I rarely find, even among some scholars, the quality of genuine faith that I have observed in many devout Jews whose simplicity was refreshing. These were some of the first generation immigrants I was privileged to know in my younger years.

The city in which I grew up would have fared much better if its shoemakers and its rabbis would have changed places. Both of our shoemakers were very quiet, unassuming people. They earned their subsistence by long hours of work in their little shops. Needless to say, not working on the *Shabbos* to increase their meager earnings was not considered a sacrifice. The idea was so absurd that it had never occurred to them.

One time the city *mikva* (ritual bath) broke down, and there was apparently a delay in getting it repaired. One of the shoemakers promptly separated from his wife, and did not return home until the *mikva* was functional again.

The other shoemaker used to listen attentively to the rabbi's learned discussions of the Talmud following afternoon services. It was questionable how much he understood.

One time, on the day following Rosh Hoshanah, he abstained from food and drink, observing the traditional Fast of G'daliah. Although he had turned eighty, the fast did not seem to bother him in the least.

After morning services he called his son at the latter's office, and told him to please come because he had something urgent to tell him. "Please, Pa," the son replied. "I have not been in the office for two days, and the work is piled up. I'll stop off on the way home tonight." But the father insisted that he had to see him promptly, and the son had no option but to leave the busy office.

Arriving at his father's home, the latter took out a manila envelope and showed the son a deed to a plot in the cemetery that he had acquired for himself many years ago. The son could not contain his anger. "For that you called me away from the office!" he shouted. "That couldn't wait until tonight? Don't you have any consideration for me?"

The father was not upset. "I just thought it was something you should know," he said.

Later that day the father attended *Mincha* and was called to read the Torah. He participated in the evening service, and went home to break his fast.

Our unsophisticated shoemaker sat down on his couch while his wife set the table, and very quietly and peacefully died.

In the Talmud, we are told that in every generation there are thirty-six pious, just men, whose true identity and virtue is secret. I suspect I may have been privileged to know two of them.

❧

Sometimes when the conversation turned to the kinds of things to which people aspire, Father would tell of a controversy that occurred in his native village of Hornostipol.

Great-grandfather, the Rebbe of Hornostipol, had a devoted attendant, Reb Dan. When the Rebbe was yet a child, he was wont to asceticism, with fasting and denying himself sleep. His grandfather, the Rebbe of Cherkassy, had assigned Reb Dan, who was several years the child's senior, to act as the latter's "big brother," and to make sure that he got adequate food and rest.

One night Reb Dan awoke after midnight, and he saw his young ward sitting on the floor, reciting the prayers of mourning for the fallen glory of Jerusalem, and shedding profuse tears for the suffering of the *Shechina,* the Divine presence, which had gone into exile along with the children of Israel.

Reb Dan warned his young ward that it was his duty to report this to the grandfather, because he had been charged with the responsibility to see that he get adequate rest. The youngster pleaded with Reb Dan not to expose him to the grandfather, whereupon Reb Dan said, "I will keep your secret on one condition. You must promise me that when you become Rebbe, you will take me as your attendant."

"What makes you think I will be Rebbe?" the child asked.

"I can foresee it," Reb Dan answered.

Reb Dan extracted the desired promise, and did not reveal the secret until the Rebbe's death some fifty years later. Reb Dan served as a faithful and devoted attendant, never leaving the Rebbe's side.

After the Rebbe's burial, the village rabbi, known as "Yankel, the Rabbi," announced that the coveted place of honor, the grave adjacent to that of the Rebbe, was due him inasmuch as he was rabbi of the village. Reb Dan protested, saying that just as he had never separated himself from the Rebbe during his lifetime, he deserved not to be separated from him in death.

The dispute was brought before Grandfather, who by then had moved from Hornostipol to Kiev. Grandfather's decision was to let the issue be decided by the Almighty; i.e., whichever of the two died first was to be buried next to the Rebbe.

Father said that whenever Yankel, the Rabbi, took ill, Reb Dan would panic. He would insist that they bring the most renowned specialists to treat him, and he would go to the synagogues to urge everyone to pray for Yankel's recovery. The thought that Yankel might predecease him and win the coveted burial place was intolerable. Conversely, if Reb Dan took sick, Yankel carried on in a similar manner.

Father would say, "Look at what some people begrudge and envy. These people had no greed for physical belongings. Their aspiration was to die first so that they would merit being near the Rebbe. They would gladly have given up years of life in order to have the burial place near the Rebbe."

Perhaps human nature has not changed. There was envy then, and there is envy now. Perhaps there is envy among all people. But the object of one's envy indicates how different the capacities of spiritual people are.

⁂

To what degree should a person be held responsible for his behavior?

In some jurisdictions, there is a legal concept of "irresistible impulse" which can be used as a defense in so-called "crimes of passion." It is apparently assumed that at a given intensity of emotion, a person's capacity to control his actions is diminished. This is consistent with the concept of man as *Homo sapiens,* or an intellectual ape; for after all, mere intellect may be grossly inadequate to restrain brute passion.

The Torah concept of man is *Adam,* a word comprised of the letter *aleph,* and the word *dam* (blood). Tradition teaches that the *aleph* represents the *Aluph,* or Master of the Universe, and *dam* is the flesh and blood physical structure of man. Man is thus not *Homo sapiens,* but *Homo spiritus,* a being whose physical self is subject to mastery of the spirit, the Divine force within him. Hence, there can be no "irresistible impulse." Even if we can understand a person's yielding to intense temptation, this does not excuse him. Man can always be in control if he so wishes; he is always responsible.

Perhaps this was the message intended in the story Father used to tell of our ancestor, Rebbe Nahum of Czernobl, the first of the Twerski family.

Following Rebbe Nahum's death, his wife would periodically visit his colleagues, fellow disciples of the Baal Shem Tov and the Maggid of Mezeritch, who helped support her.

One time,the Rebetzin visited Rebbe Boruch of Medziboz, the grandson of the Baal Shem Tov, and Rebbe Boruch asked her to relate to him some memoirs of her saintly husband.

After a few moments' thought, the Rebetzin arose and bid Rebbe Boruch farewell. In response to his astonishment at her abrupt departure, she said, "During the many years I shared with my husband, I gathered innumerable incidents of his greatness. At this very moment, not only can I not recall any of them, I cannot even retrieve his image. I take this as an indication that I do not belong here now."

Rebbe Boruch escorted the Rebetzin to her carriage. Just as the horses were about to move, she requested the driver to halt. She alighted from the carriage and said, "I recall one incident, which I have never revealed previously and would not do so now. However, since I cannot recall anything else, and this particular incident did come to my mind, I take this as an indication that this is what I am obliged to tell you.

"Rebbe Nahum and I lived in abject poverty. His entire day was spent in the study of Torah and in prayerful devotion.

"Rebbe Nahum had a pair of *tfillin* (phylacteries) which

were very dear to him. The scriptural portions contained in them had been written by Reb Ephraim, the scribe, whom the Baal Shem Tov considered to be second only to the Biblical scribes, Ezra and Nehemia. These *tfillin* were thus very special and most valuable. A wealthy member of the community had offered Rebbe Nahum fifty rubles for the *tfillin*, a sum which would have permitted our family to live in comfort for more than a year.

"However, Rebbe Nahum had said he would never part with the *tfillin*. There were times when I pleaded with him to reconsider, such as when the children had not had any food for days, or when they were cold due to lack of proper clothing, and we had no wood for the fire. I would say, 'How can you be so heartless to your own children? They need food and clothing. For two rubles, you can buy a fine set of *tfillin*, and we can then afford the essentials of life with the remainder.' But I eventually learned that all my entreaties were in vain. The *tfillin* were not negotiable.

"We were also raising our orphaned niece, Malkele, who shared our meager existence. I would say to my husband, 'When Malkele reaches marriageable age and needs a dowry, then you will sell the *tfillin*, won't you? After all, you are permitted to sell even a Torah to provide funds for a child to marry.' He would say that we would deal with that when the time came.

"One year as Rosh Hoshanah approached, it was evident that there was going to be a dearth of *esrogim** for Sukkos. For whatever reason, no *esrogim* had arrived, and my husband was terribly upset over this. The *mitzvah* of *esrog* oc-

*An *esrog* is a citrus fruit grown in tropical countries, and used ritually on the Sukkos festival (Leviticus XXXIII: 40).

curs but once a year, and to lose the opportunity to fulfill this *mitzvah* was inconceivable. He actually became depressed over this.

"On the way home from *shul* the morning of the day before Sukkos, my husband thought that from afar he saw a man carrying an *esrog* and *lulav*. Excitedly he ran after him and found this to be so. He asked the man how much he would take for the *esrog* and *lulav*, and the man responded, 'Rebbe, this is not within your means. This is the only available *esrog* in the entire region, and is for the wealthiest member of the community, who is paying fifty rubles for it.'

"Rebbe Nahum then remembered that he had been offered fifty rubles for his *tfillin*. He reasoned, 'I have already fulfilled the *mitzvah* of *tfillin* today. I will not need them again for nine days, until after Sukkos. But the *mitzvah* of *esrog* is one which I must fulfill tomorrow.' He then bade the man to wait a bit, ran off to the wealthy man, sold the *tfillin* for fifty rubles, and with the money purchased the *esrog*.

"When I returned home after trying to gather some scraps of food for the holiday, I found my husband beaming with euphoria. I inquired as to the reason for this joy, and whether perhaps he had acquired a few kopeks so that we could buy food for *Yom Tov*. But he just ignored my questions, and continued to behave as though he had found a fortune.

"I continued to press him for the reason for his joy, and he eventually told me that he had acquired an *esrog*. 'An *esrog*!' I exclaimed. 'Why, that is impossible! If there were an *esrog* available, its price would be prohibitive.' My husband reluctantly confessed that he had sold his *tfillin* in order to buy the *esrog*.

"As he said this, all the years of deprivation we had endured suddenly passed before my eyes. I saw the cold winters, when there was not a piece of firewood to mitigate the bitter frost, the children shivering in their tattered clothes. I remembered all those times the children were hungry and I had nothing to give them. But, no, he would not sell the *tfillin* then. Yet now he sells them for a piece of fruit that in eight days will be totally worthless! And what about Malkele's dowry? Malkele, my dead sister's child, whom it is my responsibility to raise and find a husband for her. Who would take her without a dowry? He sold Malkele's dowry for a piece of fruit that will be worthless in a week!

"This was more than I could bear. 'Where is the *esrog*?' I demanded. Silently, my husband pointed to the cupboard.

"In a fit of rage, I ran to the cupboard, grabbed the *esrog*, and with great force, threw it on the ground, smashing it into smithereens.

"My husband stood silent and motionless, his face ghastly pale. Two streams of tears trickled down his cheeks onto his beard.

"After a moment, he spoke. 'My precious *tfillin* I no longer have,' he said. 'The opportunity to fulfill the holy *mitzvah* of *esrog* on Sukkos I also do not have. Now Satan would wish that I lose my temper, shout at my wife, and ruin the spirit of joy on *Yom Tov*. That wish I will not grant him.' "

Rebbe Boruch listened, completely enraptured, and after a few moments of contemplation said, "Rebetzin, Rebbe Nahum loved his children no less than you did. Their suffering certainly affected him as deeply as it did you, and his concern for Malkele's welfare also equalled yours. Yet I can grasp why he did not sell the *tfillin* throughout all those years of deprivation, and I can also grasp why he did sell them to acquire the *esrog*.

"But how on earth a human being can have so great a self-mastery, not to say even a single angry word upon an act which should have provoked intense rage, that only a Rebbe Nahum could achieve."

I am sure we can sympathize with Grandmother and forgive her acting out of fury, and perhaps we are even tempted to side with her and to be critical of Grandfather's priorities.

But we are very physical people, who, in spite of what we may like to think of ourselves, are much more dominated by protoplasmic passion than by spiritual principles. I am sure that Father repeated this story so many times, not only to stimulate us to reconsider the priorities in our own lives, but even more, to make us understand that the real hero of the story is Rebbe Nahum, who had overcome the reflex response that would be so characteristic of most people and widely assumed to be the normal human response, and who became a complete master over himself, a truly free person. Not a *Homo sapiens*, but rather a *Homo spiritus*.

Rebbe Mordcha of Nesciz had longed for a *talis koton* made of wool that was produced in the Holy Land. After many efforts, he procured a piece of wool and gave it to one of his students to fashion a *talis koton* from it.

Unfortunately, in cutting out the opening, the student folded the cloth one time too many, so that instead of one hole, there were two. The student realized that he had totally ruined the garment his Master had craved so long. With great trepidation he showed Rebbe Mordcha the ruined wool, fully expecting a severe scolding for his negligence.

Rebbe Mordcha looked at the cloth very sadly, wiped away a tear from his eye, and smiled at the young man. "It's quite alright," he said. "Do not fret."

"Alright?" exclaimed the student. "But I have ruined your *talis koton*!"

"No, my child," Rebbe Mordcha said. "You see, this *talis koton* was meant to have two holes. One is for an opening for the head, and the second is to test Mordcha whether he will lose his temper."

Sometimes people intending to do *mitzvohs* may be unaware that in their fervor to perform a *mitzvah* they may transgress in other ways. Rebbe Mordcha knew that as important as the *mitzvah* of *tzizis* may be, allowing one's anger to flare would extinguish the *mitzvah*. Rebbe Mordcha had his priorities in proper order.

❧

"Oh, where is that ultimate child?" cried the Rebbe of Pscizche. "Where is that child who is driving the entire world insane?"

The Rebbe explained that in his youth, he once confronted a man who was totally immersed in his business ventures. "Why are you so totally absorbed in trying to make money? Why do you not devote more time to prayer and Torah study?"

"The man responded, 'You see, Rabbi, I really do not require that much to live on, but I must work to provide for *my child* and his future.'

"Years go by, and this child now becomes a grown man. He, too, becomes engrossed in pursuit of worldly assets. 'Why do you not take adequate time out to further your spiritual growth?' I asked of him.

"The man answered, 'I cannot, Rabbi. Although I do not need much for myself, I must provide for *my child* and his future.'

"Then *that* child grows up, and the story is again the same. It repeats itself generation after generation. No one has adequate time to devote to his own spiritual development because everyone must provide for the *child,* who in turn must provide for *his* child, and so on.

"Somewhere, then, perhaps at the end of time, there is that ultimate child, for whose welfare countless generations have so toiled that they neglected themselves in the process. Where, where is that ultimate child? Is he not but a fiction, a non-existent end-point, an illusion that has driven the entire world into an insane striving toward futility?"

A young woman had consulted me about her emotional turmoil. She felt that she was in a state of emotional paralysis, shunning any kind of relationship for fear that she would be totally engulfed by it.

"That is how it is with me," she said. "If I begin to feel, I go overboard. I have no control over my feelings and emotions. It's all or none, and I'm afraid of losing myself in my emotions."

I was reminded of a story that Father had told of the great Maggid of Mezeritch, who had been consulted by one of his disciples about the latter's helplessness to keep improper thoughts out of his mind. The Maggid advised him to consult Rebbe Wolf of Zhitomir.

The student travelled to Zhitomir, and arrived there late at night. He went to the house of Rebbe Wolf, and knocked on the door. When there was no response, he knocked louder and louder, all in vain. Since it was quite cold outside, he went around the house, knocking on the shutters, hoping to attract Rebbe Wolf's attention. But it was all for naught. There was no answer, and not knowing anyone else in Zhitomir, the student spent the night huddled in Rebbe Wolf's doorway.

As dawn broke, Rebbe Wolf opened the door, and invited the student in. After refreshing him with some hot tea, Rebbe Wolf explained. "The Maggid sent you to me to learn something. What you should learn from this encounter is that when I am master of my house, no one comes in unless I allow it, no matter how hard he may try. Similarly, you are master of your own person. No thoughts can enter your domain without your permission."

Perhaps it would be presumptuous to consider ourselves capable of achieving a self-mastery so complete that we can block unwanted thoughts from our minds, although there is really no reason why we should not try. But certainly we should not consider ourselves so weak that we have no control over our behavior.

It may actually be tempting to consider ourselves to be helpless victims of our biological drives, for this would then diminish our responsibility and accountability for our behavior. This, however, is a rationalization and nothing more. We *can* be our own masters if we really wish to be.

❧

On the long summer *Shabbos* afternoons, Father used to teach *Pirke Avos* (Ethics of the Fathers). As a child I would listen, and even if I did not understand all the intricacies, I was enchanted by the charming stories Father used to tell, parables of the Maggid of Dubnow or chassidic tales.

I recall Father questioning why the *Mishna* instructs, "Be deliberate and patient in judgment," since the ethical teachings were intended for lay people rather than for jurists. He then went on to explain that all people actually function as judges, as it were, and that we pass judgments on various matters innumerable times in our lives.

The significance of this, Father went on to say, is that just as a judge presiding over a trial is forbidden to take a bribe, so must each person be cautious and impartial. He explained that there are many factors that may impair one's capacity to judge objectively, and that the Torah states that graft so blinds a judge, that he is unaware that his judgment has been affected. Similarly, when one has ulterior motives or conflicts of interest affecting choices in his personal life, one may be totally unaware that he is not perceiving properly or not reasoning truthfully and objectively. One must therefore be in a state of constant vigilance, lest one be "bribed" into making an improper judgment in one's own life.

I don't know if this message would have impacted upon me or that I would have retained it throughout the years had it not been accompanied by the following story.

Father said that the great Rebbe of Berdichev was once sitting in a *Din Torah* (a rabbinical court), and after several days of involvement in hearing the case, he abruptly arose, announced that he must disqualify himself, and withdrew from the case. He gave no reason for his action. After *Shabbos* the Rebbe called together the other Rabbis who had been on the case with him and told them as follows.

"At one point during the proceedings of the case," the Rebbe said, "I became aware that I was losing my objectivity and was beginning to lean toward one of the litigants. Try as I might, I could not overcome this bias. I therefore had no option but to disqualify myself because of my partiality toward one side. However, I was unable to understand why this had occurred.

"On Friday night when I put on my *Shabbos* kaftan, I found in one of the pockets an envelope with money that had been placed there by one of the litigants. Apparently he had come to my home and put the money, a bribe, into one of my garments, assuming that I would find it there before issuing a judgment. He did not know that this was a garment which was reserved for use only on *Shabbos*.

"When I subsequently found the money, it became clear to me what had happened. The power of a bribe is so great, that it can influence the reasoning of a judge *even if he is unaware that he has been bribed.* From the moment that the litigant had placed the bribe in my home, my thinking began going in his favor, and I could not regain my impartiality," said the Berdichever.

I wonder, how often do we stop to consider whether the everyday decisions and judgments we render are based on a sincere desire to do what is proper and just, or whether we are perhaps "bribed" because of the apparent advantages we will obtain from a particular decision?

The capacity of the human being to rationalize is virtually endless. What is so dangerous about rationalization is that it often operates at an unconscious level. Consciously, we may actually believe we are doing something because it is the correct thing to do, whereas in truth, we are merely acting in the interests of our own convenience and pleasure. Even extreme vigilance may not be enough. One must pray, and pray hard, that he be permitted to always see the truth.

⁂

I used to hear a great deal about tightropes.

The great Rebbe of Rhizin was asked, how can one make correct decisions in one's everyday actions? It is clearly not feasible to run to an authority for guidance on every incident one encounters.

The Rhiziner answered, "Quite simple. The function of a person is to overcome temptations. The tempter is always at work, exercising his role via the cravings of one's physical being. Just as a tightrope walker maintains his balance by tilting himself to the side opposite that to which he feels pulled, so can the person make the right decision by acting opposite to that for which he feels himself craving."

Obviously, overreacting by tilting too far to any side would be lethal for the tightrope walker. I was taught of the philosophy of the Rambam (Maimonides) who taught that one should travel the "golden path," the median between two extremes. One must not be self-indulgent nor ascetic, neither a spendthrift nor a miser. Every characteristic has its two poles, and a just, well-balanced man should choose the median between these extremes. Thus spoke the Rambam, and this position was accepted as authoritative by the overwhelming majority of Jewish ethicists.

Then came along the Rebbe of Kotzk, the only existentialist whom I consider worthy of the title. Other existentialists wrote and taught existentialism. The Rebbe of Kotzk lived his existentialism at extraordinary personal sacrifice.

To the Kotzker, the only goal in life was the pursuit of truth. Truth is qualitative,not quantitative. Deviating from truth constitutes falsehood, and a little lie is no less false than a big lie. Hence, truth must always be an extreme; there can be no median between truth and falsehood.

It is characteristic of the brilliance and wit of the Kotzker that he could take an entire philosophic super-structure and demolish it with just a few words.

The golden median path did not fit into the Kotzker's existentialist scheme of things. "The middle of the road," the Kotzker observed, "is where you see all the horses travel."

❧

One of the most inspiring chassidic masters was Reb Hirsh of Rimanov. With origins in poverty and deprivation, not having had the benefit of formal schooling, he was truly a self-made man. His rule of thumb for conducting one's life has served me well.

Reb Hirsh and the great Rebbe of Rhizin united their children in marriage. Prior to the wedding, the Rebbe of Rhizin remarked, "It is customary that at a wedding we inform our children of the heritage which we transmit to them.

"My grandfather," said the Rhiziner, "was Rebbe Avrum, known as the *Malach* (angel) because of his great piety. His father was the great Maggid, the spiritual heir to the great Baal Shem Tov. On my mother's side, my grandfather was Rebbe Nahum of Czernobl,one of the most intimate disciples of the Baal Shem. On either side, our ancestry is replete with the greatest scholars in our history, and we can trace our lineage to David, King of Israel. That is our heritage which we bequeath to our children."

Reb Hirsch listened respectfully and responded quietly. "At a very young age," he said, "I was orphaned of both parents, whom I do not even recall. I survived only by the generosity of the good people in the community, who saw to it that I had food and clothing. At the age of nine, when children of my age were going to *cheder* to learn, I was apprenticed to a tailor to help with chores, and thereby to earn my keep.

"The tailor was a kind and honest man. He tried to teach me his trade, so that I could become self-supporting. He taught me, 'When you have an old garment with flaws and defects, repair it as best as you can. When you are given a piece of goods to fashion a new garment, take great caution that you do not spoil it.'

"This is my humble heritage which I can transmit to our children. Repair the flaws of the past and be cautious not to spoil the future."

⁂

Reb Chaim Cheskel was an itinerant rabbi who had come to America shortly before World War II with the hope of bringing his family over, but this wish was thwarted by the outbreak of the war.

During one of his trips through Milwaukee, Father prevailed upon Reb Chaim Cheskel to settle in Milwaukee, since I was in need of a Talmud instructor. Reb Chaim Cheskel soon acquired a number of students.

Of course, during the war there was no way of getting any news about the whereabouts of his family in Poland. One Rosh Hashona night Reb Chaim Cheskel had a frightening dream that something terrible had happened to his family. He felt compelled to fast on Rosh Hashona, and then had to comply with the unique *halacha* that if one fasts on the first day of Rosh Hashona he must fast the second day as well, and then must observe this two-day Rosh Hashona fast every year for the rest of one's life.

After the end of the war, the news of the magnitude of the terrible Holocaust began to trickle through, and Reb Chaim Cheskel knew that his nightmare had become a reality. He grieved and mourned his wife and children, but continued his function of teaching Torah to children.

One Rosh Hashona a piece of mail arrived from a Holocaust survivor who had somehow traced Reb Chaim Cheskel to Milwaukee, and confirmed what he had already known, that his wife and children had been among the millions that had perished at the hands of the Nazi beasts.

The writer added one item. Reb Chaim Cheskel's son had been assigned to work in the crematorium in Auschwitz, and had managed to smuggle in some explosives. In the hope of slowing down the mass killings and possibly saving even a few lives, he had blown himself up together with some of the crematorium equipment. Reb Chaim Cheskel wept profusely, and immediately after Rosh Hashona sat an abbreviated *shiva* (mourning period) as the *halacha* required.

Three weeks later on the festival of Simchas Torah, Reb Chaim Cheskel danced in jubilation on the rejoicing of the Torah. I looked at him with bewilderment. I was a young child, and I not only was bewildered, but also angry. I did not understand.

Now many years later, I think back about my teacher of Talmud. He was able to grieve and rejoice, to weep and dance, almost simultaneously.

Did Reb Chaim Cheskel dance because he was happy to have raised a son who gave his life for others, and did perhaps this joy overshadow the pain of the loss? I do not know for certain.

I think back upon Reb Chaim Cheskel, and even now I am bewildered. I still do not understand, but it is a bewilderment with admiration.

Reb Chaim Cheskel was a spiritual man.

What constitutes repentance? The essential and often sole ingredient in repentance is a sincere sense of regret, and this sincerity can often be achieved in even a brief moment of insight.

A student of the Rebbe of Karlin once complained to the master that he had not achieved the spiritual level and totality of devotion to which he had aspired.

"What can I do for you, my son?" the Rebbe asked. "I have thus far been unable to find the key to your heart."

"The key?" the student cried out in anguish. "Who needs a key? Use an axe to open my heart if you have to!"

"No need," the Rebbe replied. "Your heart has just opened."

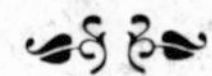

V

Self-Perspective

One Friday evening the conversation at the table turned to the *Shabbos* candles, whose kindling is in itself a beautiful way of ushering in the sacred day of rest. Lighting a candle is rich in symbolism. There are acts which we do totally for ourselves, and others which may be completely altruistic. Generating light, however, defies such limitations. I may light the candle for myself, but I cannot contain the light, because of necessity it illuminates the room for others. If I create light for the benefit of another, I too can see better.

What better way to begin the *Shabbos*, the final step in creation of the universe and its ultimate goal, than by lighting the candles, an act which symbolically binds the inhabitants of the world together. None of us can be an island; what I do affects you, and what you do must have bearing upon me. If we could only realize this, we would well understand why the candle lighting is referred to in the Rabbinic literature as an essential for *Shalom bayit*, for peace in the household. Dissension can occur only when individuals believe they are separate and distinct and can each go their own particular way, untouched by one another.

Our *Shabbos* guest asked why there were six candles burning on our table rather than the usual two. I told him it was traditional in many families to begin lighting two candles after marriage, and to add an additional candle for each child. One of the lights Mother kindled each Friday night was for me. I recall how much this had meant to me as a child, when I used to watch the flames flicker and realize that the house, nay, the world, was a brighter place because of my existence.

The full impact of this message did not occur until many years later, when it became evident to me in my psychiatric practice that countless people have emotional problems and varying psychological symptoms because of deep-seated feelings of inadequacy.

There are numerous reasons why people have unwarranted feelings of inferiority, and this is not the place to elaborate on these. Suffice it to say that anything that can be done to counteract these influences contributes to a person's sense of adequacy and wholesomeness, and allows a more satisfactory adjustment to life.

Non-verbal communications are frequently more impressive than verbal. The weekly message to a child, delivered at the initiation of *Shabbos,* that his being has brought additional brightness into the home can be a powerful ingredient in one's personality development.

One of the most deflating feelings, and one which contributes heavily to the destructive self-concept of inadequacy and unworthiness is the feeling that "I don't count." The more a person feels wanted, needed, and important, the less intense will be his negative-self feelings.

There are various ways in which a person can feel that he is important. He may feel wanted and needed by his family, friends, and community. But there is also the question of one's existence or non-existence as a whole, and the significance of this should not be minimized. Man is a thinking being, and although many modern life-styles seem to preclude indulgence in profound philosophical thinking except for a handful of contemplative scholars, there are at least fleeting moments in everyone's life when the question of one's place in the universe passes through his mind.

Humanistic philosophies, while stressing the nobility of man's interest in and service to his fellowman, fall short of providing an ultimate goal, as illustrated by the following anecdote.

A police officer once arrested two men for loitering and brought them before the judge. "What were you doing when you were arrested?" the judge asked the first man.

"Nothing," the man answered.

Turning to the second man, the judge asked, "And what were you doing?"

"I was helping him," the man said, pointing to his comrade.

As commendable as being of help and service to others is, there is an infinite regress of meaninglessness when life has no ultimate goal and purpose. Many of the practices of Jewishness, and particularly the study of Torah in its broadest and comprehensive sense, provide the individual with an indispensable reason for existence.

❧

There is a practice among chassidim that a chassid who has an audience with a Rebbe presents the latter with a *kvittl* (petition) on which he writes the names of the members of his family, followed by whatever requests he has for the Rebbe's advice or blessing.

One chassid presented such a *kvittl* to Rebbe Shneur Zalman of Liadi, the founder of Chabad. After studying the *kvittl,* the Rebbe said to his chassid, "It is apparent that you have given much thought to your needs on this earth. Have you given equal thought to why *you* are needed on this earth?"

The chassid left the Rebbe ecstatic with joy and trembling with awe. He was shaken by the Rebbe's admonishment that he had indulged too heavily in his personal concerns without giving adequate thought as to what his purpose was in the entire Divine plan of creation. Yet he was ecstatic with joy, elated with the realization that he indeed had a specific mission in the universe, one for which he specifically had been created, and one that no one else but he could fulfill. *He was needed on earth.* His being was significant, and his life had meaning.

The Psalmist says, "Rejoice with trembling" (Psalms II: 11). It is often asked, How can joy and fear co-exist? Rebbe Shneur Zalman knew how to reconcile these two apparent opposites.

❧

Quite often, patients I see in psychotherapy are dissatisfied with their lives, and many think they will find happiness by changing jobs, changing spouses, or changing locations. People seem to believe that they can achieve happiness by change, but rarely do they try to make the only change that could really be effective, which is to make a change in themselves.

As a child, I used to be lulled to sleep with stories. Mother used to tell one story whose message didn't reach me for many, many years.

There was a stonecutter who earned his livelihood by hewing out rocks from the mountain. This was backbreaking, as well as spirit-breaking work, and he would often bewail his fate. "Why was I destined to be so lowly and humble? Why are some other people so wealthy and mighty, while I break my bones every day from dawn to dusk to put bread on my table?"

One day, as he was engaged in this reverie, he heard a loud tumult in the distance. He climbed to the top of the mountain, and from afar could see a parade. The king was passing by, and on either side of the road, there were throngs of people shouting, "Bravo," and throwing flowers at the royal coach.

"How wonderful it must be to be great and powerful," the stonecutter said. "I wish that I could be king."

The stonecutter did not know that this happened to be his moment of grace, during which his wishes would be granted. He suddenly found himself transformed. He was no longer a stonecutter. He was the king, clad in ermine, sitting in the royal coach drawn by white horses, and receiving the acclaim of the crowd. "How wonderful it is to be the mightiest in all the land!"

After a bit, he began to feel uncomfortable. The bright sun was shining down on him, making him sweat and squirm in his royal robes. "What is this?" he said. "If I am the mightiest in the land, then nothing should be able to affect me. If the sun can humble me, then the sun is mightier than I. But I wish to be the mightiest of all! I wish to be the sun."

Immediately, he was transformed into the sun. He felt his mighty, unparalleled force of energy. He could give light and warmth to everything in the world. It was his energy that made vegetation grow. He could provide warmth when he so wished or devastating fires when he was angry. "I am indeed the mightiest of all," he said.

But suddenly he found himself very frustrated. He wished to direct his rays at a given point, but was unable to do so. A great cloud had moved beneath him and obstructed his rays. "Here, here!" he said. "If I am the mightiest, then nothing should be able to hinder me. If a cloud can frustrate the sun, then the cloud is mightier, yet I wish to be the mightiest. I wish to be a cloud!"

As a great, heavy cloud, he felt very powerful, dumping torrents of rain wherever he wished, and particularly when he blocked the mighty sun. But his joy was short-lived, for suddenly, he was swooped away by a sharp gust of wind against which he felt himself helpless.

"Aha!" he cried. "The wind is even mightier than a cloud! Then I shall be the wind."

Transformed into a wind, he roared over oceans, churning immense waves. He blew over forests, toppling tall trees as if they were toothpicks. "Now I am truly the mightiest," he said.

But suddenly, he felt himself stymied. He had come up against a tall mountain, and blow as he might, he could not get past. "So, " he said, "a mountain is mightier than the wind! Then I wish to be a mountain."

As a tall mountain, he stood majestically, his peak reaching above the clouds. He was indeed formidable. Neither wind nor sun could affect him. Now he was indeed the mightiest.

All at once he felt a sharp pain. What was this? A stonecutter, with a sharp pick-axe, was tearing pieces out of him. "How can this be?" he asked. "If someone can dismember me, then he must be even mightier than I. I wish to be that man." His wish was granted, and he was transformed into the mightiest of all: a stonecutter.

A while back, a young man consulted me in the office, seeking my advice regarding a choice of specialties. He was a radiology resident, but was dissatisfied with that specialty. He was considering either psychiatry or anesthesiology. Prior to radiology, he had served a year's residency in internal medicine, but did not like that specialty. Prior to medical school, he had gone to engineering college, but had left there after one year. Now he wished to know what I recommend he do.

I told the young man a story. About a stonecutter.

Rebbe Moshe of Uheli told of a dream he had, where he saw himself being led into Paradise. He was quite astonished to see Paradise as a very bland environment, and to find the sages sitting there in profound study of the Torah. Throughout his lifetime he had envisioned Heaven as something a bit more elaborate than this.

Suddenly a voice called out to him, "Moshe, son of Hanna. Do you really think the sages are in Heaven? You are mistaken. It is Heaven that is in the sages."

Rebbe Moshe awoke in the morning with a precious new bit of wisdom. Heaven and hell are not where you are, but what is within you.

Be truthful with yourself. How many times have you said, "If only I had thus and so, I would be happy."? Getting the new car and not having to spend half your life in the mechanic's garage was certainly pleasant. The new, spacious house was of course more convenient. The summer home, the outboard motor, the promotion at work, were these not perceived as the guarantors of happiness?

You know only too well what happened. Greater conveniences, yes. Happiness, not necessarily. Rebbe Moshe related his dream to us so that we do not become disillusioned and disappointed by the sense of futility resultant from looking for something in the wrong places.

◆§ §◆

Chassidic philosophy has reconciled the apparent divergent feelings of self-esteem and humility. A person must never delude himself as to his capabilities and personality endowments. Falsehood is falsehood, and a delusion of worthlessness is as fallacious and pathological as a delusion of grandiosity.

The Torah tells us that Moses was the most humble person on earth, yet there is no question that Moses did not believe himself to be an inept dullard. Moses was well aware of his enormous personality assets and of the magnitude of his achievements, but this did not interfere with his humility. If one stands before the vastness of the Pacific

Ocean, the disparity between a teaspoonful and a gallon of water is grossly diminished. In the awareness of the ever-presence of the Infinite, self-effacement is inevitable. Indeed, the greater one's grasp of Infinity, the more complete is the self-effacement.

Father used to tell of Rebbe Shneur Zalman of Liadi, who, as a student of the great Maggid of Mezeritch, once found himself perplexed by a difficult Talmudic problem, and knocked on the door of the Maggid's study to ask for enlightenment.

"Who is it?" asked the Maggid.

"It is I," Rebbe Shneur Zalman responded.

"Come in, Zalmanu," the Maggid said, recognizing the voice.

Rebbe Shneur Zalman posed his question, and after satisfactorily resolving the issue for him, the Maggid unexpectedly said, "Good-bye, Zalmanu. Have a good journey," and dismissed him.

Rebbe Shneur Zalman was perplexed. Good-bye? A journey? Where to? But it was not for him to ask. The Maggid had instructed him to go, so he picked up his *talis* and *tfillin* and began traveling.

He hiked far beyond Mezeritch, and as he made his way along the countryside, he heard from afar the cry, "Hey, there, you! Come here!"

From afar, Rebbe Shneur Zalman saw an isolated house, and someone standing beside it beckoning to him. As he approached, several people welcomed him. "You are a Godsend," they said. "We are celebrating a *bris* (circumcision), and we would like to have a *minyan* (quorum of ten men). We are only nine, and you are the tenth."

After the *bris*, the group sat down to a festive meal, and

invited Rebbe Shneur Zalman to join with them. After the meal was over, Rebbe Shneur Zalman was about to leave, when the mistress of the house announced that in counting the silverware, one silver spoon was missing. Immediately, all eyes turned to the stranger.

The master of the house approached Rebbe Shneur Zalman. "Look," he said, "we are grateful to you for completing the *minyan*, and if you wish, we will give you some alms, but stealing silver is not acceptable. Please return the spoon."

"But I did not take any spoon," Rebbe Shneur Zalman protested.

"We know all our friends here as honest men," the master said. "It could not be anyone other than you who has taken it. Give it back!"

"It was not I," Rebbe Shneur Zalman again protested.

"You are a liar as well as a thief," the master said. "You are the thief."

"Not I," Rebbe Shneur Zalman said.

"Yes, you," the master said, this time accompanying his words with a rough shove.

"No, not I," Rebbe Shneur Zalman said. Soon the group gathered around him, shouting at him, and then beating him, while he vainly protested repeatedly, "Not I."

After awhile, the maid, unable to watch an innocent man being beaten, confessed that she had stolen the silver spoon. The group then apologized to Rebbe Shneur Zalman and sent him on his way.

Rebbe Shneur Zalman then reflected, "Obviously, I was sent away by the Maggid because for some reason I had deserved a punishment for something. Now that I have collected what was due me, I may certainly return," and he directed his steps back towards Mezeritch.

The Maggid was waiting for him at the door. "Nu, Zalmanu," he said. "How many times did you have to shout, 'Not I'?

"You see," the Maggid continued, "when you knocked on my door and I asked who it was, you answered, 'It is *I*.' Zalmanu, there is only one Being in the universe who has the right to say. 'It is *I*.' *Anochi Hashem Elokecha, I* am the Lord thy God. A human being should always be aware of himself as standing in the presence of God. This should result in a total *bittul* (self-effacement). Under such circumstances, there can be no concept of one's self being an *I*. Your statement, 'It is I,' was inappropriate and something which you had to undo. Divine Providence gave you the opportunity to do so. Just see how many times you have to repeat, 'It is *not* I,' to undo a single inappropriate self-assertion of 'It is I.' "

The greater the clarity and purity of a precious stone, the more noticeable and unacceptable is even the minutest defect. The lack of total self-effacement for which the Maggid admonished Rebbe Shneur Zalman was a fault only for someone as great as the latter, whose enormous wisdom and profound grasp of Divine Infinity rendered the simple statement, "It is I," a transgression.

Humility and greatness are not disparate. They are one and the same.

❧

As a psychiatrist, I have advocated the need for a positive self-image as a vital ingredient for mental health, pointing out that people with poor self-esteem, who see themselves negatively, are apt to have many psychological and emotional problems.

At times I have been challenged that this is in contradiction to Torah teaching, which emphasizes the importance of humility and self-effacement.

I had never considered these two positions as incompatible, and perhaps this was because I saw them both unified in Father.

As a community leader, teacher, personal counselor, and healer of souls, Father was without peer. He would advise people on issues that crucially affected their lives, and was able to do so because he was completely confident that his advice was sound. There was no doubt that he was well aware of his enormous capacities.

Yet, if anyone wished for a model of humility, it was Father. In no way did he ever feel superior to anyone else. His total involvement with anyone who sought his help was without condescension.

When events occurred at which there was protocol as to who would be seated in the foremost spaces, who would speak first, who would be accorded certain honors, Father would laugh at this. He was amused by those who struggled for special recognition. To him this meant nothing at all, and if he had any input into the arrangements, he would always place himself last. When the sages said "He who flees from fame and recognition will be pursued by them," they were speaking of Father. He had no desire for acclaim, and it pursued him relentlessly.

The person who is grandiose and thirsts for external recognition is invariably one who needs the esteem of others because he has so little of his own. In Father I saw not only the compatibility of self-esteem with humility, but their absolute identity.

⁂

Although many of the chassidic Rebbes used parables to drive home a point, the master of story-telling was Rebbe Nachman of Bratzslav. His stories are often quite entwined, very complex, yet most enchanting, and lend themselves to multiple interpretations. It is said that Franz Kafka was inspired by the stories of Rebbe Nachman.

Mother would often relate some of the stories and offer her own interpretations.

One brief story stands out in my memory. A king was once informed by his chief minister that there had been a blight on the crops of that year, which had been so affected that anyone who would eat of the grain would become insane. "But," said the minister, "there is no need for us to worry. I have set aside enough grain from last year's harvest for the both of us that will last us until the harvest of the following year."

The king shook his head. "No," he said. "I will not give myself any special privileges other than those shared by my subjects.

"We shall all eat of the same grain," the king continued. "But here is what we shall do. You and I will mark our foreheads with an indelible imprint, so that when we go insane, I will look at you and you will look at me, and *we will know.*"

I cannot be certain what Rebbe Nachman intended with this story. What I derived from this is that in an insane world, no one is immune. But sometimes, sanity consists of recognizing that one is insane.

I do not know whether the world was always as chaotic as it is now. I suspect that the enormous advances in technology, while giving us many conveniences, have exacted an exorbitant price. Our ancestors, lacking the means of rapid travel and instantaneous communications, undoubtedly lived more serene lives. Today we measure our lives in seconds if not milliseconds. We risk our own lives, as well as others, by rushing through a yellow traffic light. Pre-prepared instant foods, microwave ovens, and supersonic jets have eroded, if not completely eradicated, our tolerance for any delay. We are under frequent pressure to meet deadlines of our own making. We have developed a life style of rushing that is so pervasive that we sometimes rush without really knowing why we are doing so or even what it is we are rushing for.

During Father's last illness, I sat with him in his hospital room. He was looking out the window and watching the busy traffic, and the throngs of pedestrians. Cars were weaving in and out, trying to gain a nonsensical advantage of twenty feet, and some were screeching to a halt for pedestrians who were running across the street, dodging oncoming cars. Father turned to me and smiled. "A foolish world," he said.

Rebbe Bunim of Pscizche once observed someone pacing to and fro. "Pardon me," he said to the man, "but I am curious about something. I can understand why you went from here to there, because perhaps things are better there than here. I can also understand why you returned, because on arriving there you realized things were really better here. What I cannot understand is why you went back there again."

We are often so caught up in the torrid pace that surrounds us, that we do not realize how senseless some of our behavior is. We have become victims of a life style which exacts so much from our systems that we fall victim to many diseases that are caused by stress.

Ideally, we should change some of our behavior. An important first step is to realize that we may have been so caught up in the insanity of our culture, that we think this life style to be normal. Rebbe Nachman was right. We need to recognize insanity, even if it is so prevalent that everyone assumes it is normal.

☙ ❧

The following story has undoubtedly been recorded elsewhere, yet I include it here because it emphasizes the theme on which I expounded in my book, *Like Yourself and Others Will, Too,* namely, that many people are grossly unaware of their own personal strengths and resources. Indeed, I believe that many emotional behavioral disorders are a result of this distortion of the self-perception.

In Cracow, there stands a *shul* known as "The Shul of Izik Reb Yekale's." The story goes that Izik was a peasant who had a repetitious dream. Again and again he dreamed that under a particular bridge in Prague there lie buried a huge treasure, which would belong to anyone who unearthed it. At first Izik dismissed the dream as an absurdity, but after numerous repetitions he began to take it more seriously.

Yet the whole thing was so preposterous. How was he, Izik, who did not have two copper coins to rub together, to get to Prague? But the obsession gave him no rest, and although his wife told him to get the crazy idea out of his head, he decided once and for all that he must go to Prague and find the treasure. So, one day, he took some meager provisions and set out for Prague.

When Izik was fortunate enough to hitch a ride on a passing wagon, he rode. Otherwise, he hiked, begging for handouts of food at inns along the way, and sleeping in the shelter of the trees.

After many weeks, Izik arrived at Prague, and sought out the bridge he had envisioned in his dream. But alas, there were always police patrolling the area, and there was no way he could begin to dig.

Day after day, he loitered around the bridge, hoping that perhaps there would be a break in the patrol, and he would be able to dig for the treasure. Finally one of the police patrols approached him. "Why are you constantly loitering around this area day after day?" the policeman asked. "What is it that you want here?"

Izik saw no other way than to simply tell the truth. He related his repetitious dream to the policeman, and also the weeks of travail until he came to Prague from his humble village near Cracow.

The policeman howled with laughter. "You fool!" he said. "And because of a silly dream you came all the way here? Well, I have had a repetitious dream, too. I have been dreaming that in a tiny village near Cracow, there is a little hut that belongs to a peasant named Izik Reb Yekale's, and that under the floor of that hut there lies buried an immense treasure."

The story goes that Izik immediately returned home from Prague, and upon digging up the earthen floor of his hut, discovered an immense treasure. It was out of this fortune that the Shul of Izik Reb Yekale's was built.

Many people look for wealth elsewhere. They search for wealth of all kinds, but especially for the greatest wealth of all: happiness. They think that it is to be found elsewhere, and they expend enormous energies to search it out. Little do they know that the happiness they seek lies right within themselves. No need to travel long distances or to work in foreign territories. It is there at one's fingertips, right within one's self. One only has to believe this and to look within.

❧

My clinical emphasis on the importance of attaining a positive self-concept and avoiding self-flagellation may have had its origin in an anecdote about the *Chafetz Chayim* (Rabbi Israel Meir HaCohen) which Father repeated many times.

The *Chafetz Chayim* had gained great renown as a sage through his *halachic* works and especially through his campaign against gossip and slander.

One time the *Chafetz Chayim* was returning to his home in Radin, when his coach passed a man walking along the road. The *Chafetz Chayim* had the driver stop, and offered the man a ride to Radin.

Once aboard, the man struck up a conversation and said that he was on his way to Radin to see the great *zaddik*, the *Chafetz Chayim*.

The *Chafetz Chayim* shrugged his shoulders. "I don't know why you are making all that effort," he said. "There is nothing special to see in that man. He really looks just like everyone else."

The man became enraged. "How dare you speak with such disrespect about the greatest *zaddik* of our generation!" he shouted, and in his rage slapped the *Chafetz Chayim* in the face.

Later in Radin when the man came to greet the *Chafetz Chayim* and recognized that this was the person whom he had slapped, he fell before his feet and asked for forgiveness.

The *Chafetz Chayim* smiled. "Forgiveness? There is no

need for forgiveness," he said. "After all, it was my honor you were defending. But I did learn something new from this experience. I have always pointed out how wrong it is to belittle others. Now, I know it is also wrong to belittle oneself."

In my psychiatric practice, I found that a multitude of emotional problems are due to people having an unwarranted low self-esteem. Many faulty adjustments to life can be directly attributed to the distortion of the self-concept which afflicts so many people.

It should be obvious that a person could not possibly adapt appropriately to reality if, for whatever reason, he misperceives reality. One's own self is certainly a part of reality. Misperception of the self cannot but result in serious maladjustments.

In these cases, psychotherapy should be directed primarily to helping the individual achieve a correct self-awareness. Unfortunately, many psychotherapists too often focus on searching for pathology, for childhood deprivation and trauma, for whatever went wrong in the patient's life. This may at times be futile, and the patient would fare better if he were helped to get a true picture of himself, and find out what is *right* with him instead of what is wrong.

The Rebbe of Kotzk knew this well. He once challenged a newcomer to his court with, "Young man, why have you come here?"

"I have come to discover God," answered the young man.

"Then you have made an unnecessary trip, young man," the Rebbe said. "God is present everywhere. You could have discovered him right at home."

"Then why should I have come?" the young man asked.

"To discover yourself, young man," the Rebbe of Kotzk said. "To discover yourself."

⁂

The problem of unwarranted low self-esteem is not exclusive to the individual. There are families who manifest low self-esteem as a unit, and this can be true of communities and entire nations as well.

One of the many unfortunate consequences of Jews having lived among hostile populations is that many Jews have developed an "exile complex", manifested by self-effacement and subservience.

I was once traveling on a bus, dressed in my customary garb, wearing a broad black hat and a black frock coat. A man approached me and said, "I think it's shameful that your appearance is so different. There is no need for Jews in America to be so conspicuous, with long beards and black hats."

"I'm sorry, mister," I said to the man. "I'm not Jewish. I'm Amish, and this is how we dress."

The man became apologetic. "Oh I'm terribly sorry, sir," he said. "I did not mean to offend you. I think you should be proud of preserving your traditions."

"Well, well," I said. "If I am Amish, then my beard and black hat doesn't bother you, and I should be proud of my traditions. But if I am Jewish, then I must be ashamed of my Jewishness? What is wrong with you that you can respect others but have no self-respect?"

The time has certainly arrived when we ought to be proud of our heritage, of who we are, why we are, and what we are for.

⁂

VI

The Festivals

Some of my most cherished memories relate to the *yomim tovim* (holidays), and I was fortunate that the modern super-industrialized commercialism had not deprived me of these experiences.

The joy of Chanukah actually began several days before the holidays. Father would use a beeswax candle to light the wicks of the oil burning *menorah* (candelabra), and since beeswax candles were unavailable commercially, he would make them himself, eight of them, one for each night. He would also make one extra candle to put away for use in the search for *chometz* (leavened bread) on the night before Passover.

Father would buy a large cake of beeswax, and cut it into small squares. I was permitted to take a few of the sweet-smelling chips and play with them as with moulding clay. Then he would soften the wax in a pan of hot water, flatten them, place a thick string in the center for a wick, and roll them into thin cylinders.

After Father lit the Chanukah candles, he would sit and observe them for a half-hour, while chanting some of the Psalms with a melody reserved for Chanukah.

Mother of course served potato *latkes* on Chanukah, but I also had an extra treat. The members of the ladies' auxiliary of our *shul* had an annual Chanukah event, at which they served buckwheat pancakes. I was also the recipient of their bounty of candy and chewing gum.

Aromas and fragrances can be powerful memory stimulants. Even today, the fragrance of *challah* as it browns in the oven on Fridays transports me back to the Fridays of my childhood when the steaming, fresh *challah*, dipped into the hot broth of freshly cooked gefilte fish, constituted the ultimate in gourmet foods.

The gifts that I received as a child on Chanukah have long since returned to the elements. I cannot recall a single toy I received on Chanukah. But I can still relive the candle-making, and when really well-relaxed in reverie, I can even smell the melted beeswax. I can see myself sitting on Father's lap and watching the Chanukah lights glow.

The miracle of Chanukah was that a tiny bit of oil lasted for eight days. An even greater miracle is that the glow of Father's Chanukah lights have lasted for five decades.

❧

Of all occasions, Passover is the king of childhood memories.

Passover is the children's holiday. The ritual of the Seder is totally centered about children. The children initiate the Seder by reciting the four questions to elicit the response of the narration of the Exodus. Many Seder rituals are performed specifically to stimulate the curiosity of children. And it is the children's role to "steal" the *matzah* (unleavened wafers) and hold it until it is ransomed with cherished prizes.

In more ways than one, Passover is the much sought-after fountain of youth. One never outgrows one's identity as a child in relation to Passover. According to *halacha,* even if one is old and totally alone, he must begin the Seder with asking the four questions. Asking of whom? Why, God, of course! We are never without a father. If one is not in the company of children, one becomes the child oneself.

The *Haggadah* (account of the Exodus) states, "In every generation, a person must view oneself as having personally participated in the Exodus from Egypt, emancipated from slavery." Just as the individual can recapture his childhood, so must the nation re-experience its infancy. Individually and collectively, Passover is a rejuvenation.

It is one of the ironies of life that as children we wish to be grownups, and when we finally do grow up, we wish we could be children again. Passover allows us to be both child and adult.

I recall the excitement of cleaning the house for Passover. I would help with carrying out the many volumes of Father's library, and shaking out the books on the porch in the open air. Heaven forbid that while someone was reading one of the books at the table, a crumb of bread might have fallen among the pages. I would also help with carrying up the Passover dishes from the cellar. The most beautiful dishes were always set aside for Passover. I had a tiny silver wine cup which was all mine.

The night before Passover, we followed Father around the house as he carried the beeswax candle, searching for any *chometz* that might have escaped the vigorous cleaning of the past few weeks. Mother had followed the tradition of placing ten little pieces of bread in secret places around the house, to make sure that Father thoroughly searched all the rooms, because not until he had accounted and retrieved all of the ten pieces would the search be completed. Of course, I had been with Mother when she hid the pieces, but never revealed the hiding places to Father. If he found only nine of the ten, he would have to continue searching the entire house for the tenth piece. I knew the secret, but would never have revealed it. And the following morning, we watched the bonfire as Father threw in whatever *chometz* had remained.

Father used to convert some all-year-round utensils for Passover use. He would put them into a pail of boiling water, and then throw a red-hot brick into the water that would send up a geyser like Old Faithful. What fun!

On the morning before Passover, we ate in the cellar, since all of the rooms in the house had been sanitized for Passover. Danish pastries never tasted as delicious on any occasion as they did in the cellar on that day.

I was fortunate in having a special treat, because on the day before Passover, we baked our own *matzah* for the Seder. Nothing in the world is as exciting as baking *matzah*.

The evening before the Seder night, we would drive out to the country where there was a fresh-water spring to fetch water for baking the *matzah*. Father would take out his pocket watch, and we would wait until precisely the moment of sunset to begin filling the glass jugs, because that is when the water is at its coolest, as it must be to avoid the flour being soured by warm water. Did you ever taste delicious water? Try the spring water on the evening before the Seder. (It helps, incidentally, if you are six or seven years old.)

After we brought the jugs into the house, the men would form a circle and dance to the tune of "And Ye Shall Fetch Water with Joy from the Wells of Salvation" (Isaiah 12:5), while balancing the water jugs on their shoulders. The actual baking of the *matzah* did not begin until noontime the following day, corresponding to the time of the Paschal lamb ritual in the days of yore. Since I was not yet Bar-Mitzvah, I was not permitted to participate in the actual baking of the *matzah,* but there were plenty of things for me to do. I cleaned the rolling pins with sandpaper and delivered fresh sheets of butcher paper to the men who were rolling the *matzah* dough.

All this was supervised by Reb Elia, a Jerusalemite who used to visit us every Passover. Reb Elia was the sweetest man on earth, but on the day before Passover, he underwent a metamorphosis and was an absolute tyrant when it came to the *matzah* baking. Everything had to be done with haste and precision, lest anyone cause a momentary hesitancy in preparation of the dough. Beware! Reb Elia's voice thundered across the room, instilling the fear of God into everyone.

A voice would ring out, "A *matzah* for the oven!" as one of the men would near completion of his *matzah* dough. "A *matzah* for the oven!" I would repeat, running to tell Reb Saul to prepare the long pole wherewith he would transfer the *matzah* into the oven.

After the baking was completed, the men joined hands and danced in a circle. There was true joy. We had just completed preparation for the once-a-year *mitzvah* of *matzah.* "Next year in Jerusalem!" went the refrain.

We returned home with boxes of freshly-baked *matzah,* to the once-a-year menu of fluffy potato dumplings and borscht. I have never tried to repeat this menu during the year. It couldn't possibly taste the same.

The long day was exhausting, but a six- or seven-year-old seems to have infinite reserves of energy. Yet, sometime during the Seder, particularly after a few sips of wine, I would get drowsy, and sit with Father on the big couch, which Mother had draped with a golden bedspread and padded with huge pillows. I would rest my head on Father's lap, and the tunes of the *Haggadah* were my lullaby. I would drift off into a sweet sleep, which could have been experienced only one other time in the history of the universe: that of Adam in Paradise.

My children are now grown and have children of their own. On Passover, my grandchildren enjoy the Passover excitement as I once did. My reserves of energy are far less than they were in those days. I now sit on the draped couch, and my grandchildren put their heads on my lap, and enjoy that sweet sleep.

I identify with my grandchildren. I know what they feel and how they feel. It is much more than a vicarious gratification, for I am once again the child, falling asleep on Father's lap as he chants, "Who Knows What Is One? One is the Almighty Who Rules over Heaven and Earth." Passover allows me to be a child once again, in spite of the grey hairs in my beard.

No one knows what awaits them later in life, but whatever and wherever, I will always have Passover with me.

⁂

One childhood experience that related to Passover was most helpful to me many years later.

Preparation of food on Passover was not much of a

problem. All the dishes and utensils used were exclusively for Passover, and the kitchen was completely cleaned and outfitted for Passover purposes. Not so with the preparation of *schmaltz* (chicken fat) for Passover.

Passover *schmaltz* was made from goose fat rather than chicken fat, and the season for geese was around Chanukah time. Preparing a Passover item in an environment that was full of *chometz* was not a simple task. One small area of the kitchen was scoured and the kitchen counters covered with boards, and two of the burners on the stove were converted for Passover use. The dining room table was covered with heavy butcher paper, and on these three specially prepared areas the *schmaltz* was processed in a few Passover utensils that had been brought up from the basement.

Since everything else in the house was *chometz'dig*, anyone coming in contact with the Passover area or utensils had to use great caution not to touch anything that was *chometz'dig*, otherwise they would become "contaminated," and thereby contaminate or ruin the Passover *schmaltz*. If there was accidental contact with anything *chometz'dig*, the person would have to promptly scrub his hands before touching any Passover item.

The whole experience was an exciting one for me as a child, if only because it was a harbinger that the coveted Passover holiday was soon approaching, even though it was still several months away.

Many years later as a medical student, my colleagues and I were introduced to the surgical suite. We were told that only a very circumscribed area is considered surgically sterile: the operating table, the instrument table, and the area of one's own person between the waist and the shoulders. Touching anything outside of this area, such as raising one's hand to adjust the face mask, constituted a break in sterile technique which "contaminated" the person and necessitated rescrubbing, regowning, and regloving.

I noticed that many of my colleagues had some difficulty in adjusting to this degree of discipline. To me it came naturally. Surgical sterility is just like making Passover *schmaltz*. Little had I known that at age six, I was being prepared for proper surgical technique.

⁂

The seventh night of Passover was a special event. Inasmuch as the seventh day of Passover commemorated the miracle of the Israelites crossing the Red Sea, people would gather at our home after the evening meal to join in the Song of Triumph which had been composed by Moses.

Reb Elia, who had presided over the *matzah* baking, led the group in responsive reading. Reb Elia's voice thundered with resonance, but this time in an attitude of joy and celebration, rather than stern discipline.

After completion of the reading of the song of Moses, the group joined hands and danced in a circle, to the lively melody of "When You Divided the Red Sea, Your Nation Saw Your Might and Glory."

The identification with our ancestors who had participated in the miraculous crossing of the sea once grew so intense that one of the group ran off and brought a bucket of water, and poured it onto the floor where we were dancing. Mother was not at all pleased with this attempt to simulate the historic experience. I thought it was hilarious!

⁂

The following story, which is but one of the many miraculous tales of the chassidic masters, is being recorded simply because I was fortunate to hear it directly from two distinct eyewitness participants, and my father knew countless other eyewitnesses to the event. Hence, it is an authentic account, and it would be a shame to allow it to be lost to posterity.

As a young boy, I knew Zelig Chepovetsky, then a man in his late seventies. Zelig was a native of Ivankov, a small town in the Ukraine near Kiev. Great-grandfather, the Rebbe of Hornostipol, also near Kiev, was accepted as the ultimate authority for religious matters in the nearby towns.

Zelig's father was known as Moshe the Professor. This came about because Moshe, who was unable to earn a living, once bemoaned his plight to the Rebbe, whose response was, "Go become a doctor."

To Moshe, the Rebbe's word was law. Since learning medicine formally was out of the question, Moshe hired himself out to the local physician as an apprentice, and carried the doctor's medical bag. He would observe the patients' symptoms and make note of what the doctor prescribed for each malady. After a while, he began treating patients himself, and lo and behold! Moshe's treatments seemed infallible: all his patients recovered. His fame spread, and the most prominent doctors in Kiev proudly referred to Moshe as "our esteemed colleague."

The major industry of Ivankov was the manufacture of yeast, and several of the yeast factories were of Jewish ownership. Since on Passover, Jewish ownership of yeast is forbidden, the proprietors would sign a contract giving title to their factories to non-Jews, and then continue to operate the factories during Passover.

The Rebbe strongly condemned this practice since he considered the contract to be a sham. Yet, the practice continued year after year. One time on the *Shabbos* prior to Passover, when the residents of the nearby towns gathered at the Rebbe's, he reprimanded the Ivankovites for disobeying his wishes, and said, "Remember, the *halacha* states that *chometz* which is retained on Passover must be destroyed by fire."

Moshe the Professor, also an Ivankovite, who was among those assembled cried out, "But, Rebbe, I am not at fault. I have nothing to do with manufacturing yeast." To which the Rebbe replied, "I did not mean you, Moshe."

Zelig told me that late in the afternoon on the eve of Passover, a fire erupted in the town and spread very rapidly. The townsfolk tried to save some of their belongings by taking them across the river which divided the town, but the fire jumped the river and destroyed every house in the village, with but one exception, Moshe's house.

Grandfather told me that on that Passover eve, his father, the Rebbe, appeared very agitated, and delayed the celebration of the Seder. In the midst of the Seder, the doors flew open, and a delegation of the Ivankov townsfolk, Zelig among them, came to report to the Rebbe that they had lost everything in the fire.

The Rebbe sent word throughout his community for everyone to keep only minimum rations for themselves, and to send all the food that could be spared to Ivankov. A caravan of wagons was organized to carry provisions, furnishings, and bedclothes to the ravaged city.

Some sixty years later, Zelig related this story to me, the tears streaming down his cheeks. "Yes," he said, "the Rebbe destroyed our town. But he also rebuilt it."

Father did not demand that his children become practicing rabbis. However, in the event we did, he let us know that being a good rabbi required more than book knowledge. In order to render any opinion or judgment, the rabbi must be capable of making a comprehensive assessment of a situation. He must be able to see beneath the surface.

Father loved to tell the story of one of the citizens of his Ukrainian village, Hornostipol. Boruch Yochanan was a very pious albeit simple Jew who came to Yankel, the village rabbi, on the eve of Passover, with the problem that his wife had just told him that she had accidentally cooked the Seder meal in a *chometz'dige* pot. The rabbi responded that there was no way out. The food was forbidden to be used and must be discarded.

Boruch Yochanan brought the sad judgment home to his wife. Not having anything to eat, they went to join Great-grandfather at his Seder.

Great-grandfather of course welcomed them graciously, but then asked why they were not having a Seder of their own. Boruch then explained about the mishap of the food being cooked in the *chometz'dige* pot, and that Yankel, the rabbi had condemned it.

"What!" exclaimed Great-grandfather. "Yankel ruled it forbidden? Did you throw it away already?"

Boruch's wife admitted that she had not yet discarded the food, but had immediately taken off with her husband to Great-grandfather's house.

"Then go home and make your Seder, and eat your meal in good health!" Great-grandfather said. Boruch and his wife quickly complied.

In the meantime, it slowly occurred to Yankel, the rabbi, that since he had ruled the food to be forbidden, Boruch would have nothing to eat for the Seder. He therefore had his wife take several portions from the food they had prepared for themselves and send it by messenger to Boruch's home.

By the time the messenger made the delivery to Boruch's home, the latter and his wife were already partaking of their own food. Boruch then explained to the messenger that the Rebbe had overruled Yankel, and the messenger then carried the food back.

Yankel was perplexed. How could the Rebbe have overruled him, since there was no dissent in the ruling that food cooked in a *chometz'dige* pot was forbidden? He left his Seder and went to Great-grandfather.

Grandfather did not wait for Yankel to pose the question. "Yankel, Yankel," he said. "Where is your common sense? Don't you know how Boruch's wife prepares for Passover? Don't you know that three days before Passover, all the *chometz'dige* pots and dishes have been put away? Don't you realize that it is a physical impossibility for there to have been a *chometz'dige* pot in Boruch's kitchen on the afternoon before Passover?"

"But Boruch said . . ." Yankel protested.

"So he said! So you ask, Yankel," Great-grandfather said. "You know, there is a practice that women have adopted, that the pot that is used to boil eggs on Passover is not used for anything else. Colloquially, the egg pot has been given the name "the *chometz'dige* pot" even though it is strictly for Passover use. Go ask Boruch's wife, Yankel, and she will tell you. I did not even ask. I simply knew there was no way on earth for there to be an actual *chometz'dige* pot in Boruch Yochanan's kitchen on the day before Passover."

So Father used to tell us that before passing judgment on

anything or anyone, we must have a thorough understanding of the real facts, rather than the facts which we are given.

When I began learning how to take a good psychiatric history from a patient, I was told that the data presented may appear to be factual, but can be very misleading. A good psychotherapist must have a comprehensive grasp of the whole of the patient's life before he can understand all its components.

There are excellent psychotherapists who, like Great-grandfather, can see through words. There are others, who like Yankel, mistakenly assume that words have an independent validity.

⁂

As a rabbi, as a psychiatrist, or in any capacity where one's counsel is sought, it is important to know what people want or need when they ask questions. Sometimes they are looking for answers, and they really want an opinion. At other times, they have already come to a conclusion, but wish to hear their decision confirmed by an authority.

Many people know the solutions to their problems more thoroughly than any outside authority. Yet, they may be uncertain that their decisions are correct. They may feel that their reasoning may have been influenced by one or more emotions. They may already have the right answers to problems, but need confirmation that their decisions are indeed correct.

Yankel, the village rabbi, seems not to have been the wisest of men.

Father told of one time when there was a festive occasion

at Great-grandfather's home, attended by many learned rabbis of the nearby villages. During the dinner, someone serving the chicken noted that in one portion, the thigh bone of the chicken had been fractured and had mended. According to *halacha,* certain injuries sustained by the animal or bird can render it *trefa* (prohibited for consumption). Great-grandfather and a number of the rabbis inspected the bone and concluded that it was a benign condition, but Great-grandfather nevertheless insisted that inasmuch as Yankel was the official rabbi of the community, his opinion must be sought.

A messenger carried the specimen in question to Yankel. How shocked everyone was when the messenger returned with Yankel's ruling: *trefa*! Great-grandfather immediately ordered all the food to be removed from the table, and all the utensils which had come in contact with the condemned fowl to be *kashered* (ritually cleansed).

The rabbis in attendance were furious. How stupid of Yankel to make so obvious an error! They went to Yankel's home and berated him for his ignorance.

With head hung low in shame, Yankel came to Great-grandfather to confess his mistake.

Great-grandfather shook his head in compassion. "Yankel," he said, "there is nothing reprehensible about overlooking a particular point of law. We all make mistakes at one time or another.

"But lack of *sechel* (common sense) is something altogether different. Just think a bit, Yankel. If the correct ruling would have been *trefa,* would we have asked for your opinion? You should have understood that since we were all partaking of the meal, and hence we had a personal interest that the ruling be kosher, I refused to accept a positive decision from anyone who was personally involved. I therefore requested your opinion as an uninterested party. I wouldn't have needed your opinion if it were *trefa*. Yankel, we didn't send you a *question;* we sent you the *answer*, but you didn't understand this."

Answers are appropriate responses only to propositions that are questions. Answers given to propositions that are grammatically questions but contextually statements are never satisfactory.

There are other times when what appears to be a question in syntax is actually a rationalization. In fact, it is just the opposite of a question, since no answer is acceptable.

This little story must be told in Yiddish, since the particular play on words is unique to Yiddish. The Hebrew word, *terutz,* which means an answer to a question, is also used in Yiddish to mean an "excuse" or a "rationalization".

A man once came to a rabbi and said that he had many questions on the Torah. He had found many internal contradictions and other inconsistencies. The rabbi heard him out and said, "I cannot give you any answers, because you did not pose any questions. In fact, the questions you raised are not questions, but *terutzim* (literally "answers", but colloquially "excuses"). You see, you really do not wish to abide by the many restrictions on behavior imposed by the Torah. However, rather than simply defying the Torah, you have found a way to ease your conscience. You have therefore come up with questions or challenges to the Torah, because if you can demonstrate that the Torah is somehow incorrect, you will feel justified in not adhering to its demands. You need a *terutz* (excuse) for why you do forbidden things on *Shabbos,* so you have come up with a question on the Torah. You wish to indulge in non-kosher food, and you need a *terutz* for doing so, so you come up with a question, which would serve to disprove the authenticity of the Torah. I can provide *terutzim* (answers) when they are sought as response to legitimate questions, but your questions are *terutzim* (excuses) by themselves, and no answer will satisfy you."

This principle has been most helpful to me in my psychiatric practice. What the rabbi said is very true. If you find that an answer does not satisfy a question, it is likely that the question is not a question at all.

As an example, I recall a young man who consulted me because of a persistent depression. He felt completely unmotivated to do anything with his life. He had excellent opportunities to develop a career, whether in a trade or profession, but he felt paralyzed. He said that three years earlier he had been engaged to a young lady, but her parents objected to the marriage and she broke off the engagement. She had since married, but he has never been able to go on with anything because life is no longer meaningful. He posed a question, "Why am I unable to get over her?"

I spent several hours with him, analyzing why he was not able to put that relationship behind him. Most people eventually do get over a rejection just as they do over any other loss. We investigated many reasons. All sounded plausible, but none reached him emotionally.

That night I had a dream. I was back at a bungalow where I spent the summer when I was ten. I used to love to row, but was not permitted to take a boat out on the lake unless I was accompanied by an adult. I therefore used to go down to the pier, and while the boat was tied fast to the pier, I would row to my heart's content. This was the scene I dreamt.

I awoke with the awareness that I had found the solution

to the young man's problem. The way he saw it was that he was unable to go on with his life *because* he was still attached to this first relationship. Actually, the reverse was true. He was a very insecure person, afraid to try anything because he was convinced he would fail. He therefore *tied* himself to this first relationship and refused to let go, just as I tied my boat to the pier so that I would not go out onto the lake. The relationship was not holding onto him, but rather *he* was holding on to *it*.

Many times in our lives we feel we have questions, and we are frustrated because we cannot get satisfactory answers. It would be well to examine these questions and see whether they are really questions, or rather *terutzim*. There are satisfactory answers to questions, but there are no answers to *terutzim*.

⸻

Passover just dripped with tradition. Every bit of the ritual, especially of the Seder, was performed by Father just as he had seen it done by his father, and so on *ad infinitum*. As a child I could have sworn that whoever conducted the first Seder in history did it exactly the way Father did. How could it be otherwise? It was a shocking revelation when I discovered that there were customs other than ours. But when I made this discovery I was already firmly entrenched in Father's way of doing things.

That is the strength of tradition: it provides a protective bulwark against erosion. Whatever has remained of Torah observance is attributable to the strength of tradition, and on the insistence that even apparent trivia be considered sacrosanct.

Father used to tell of a very simple man, just barely literate, who came to a bookstore asking to buy a *sidur*. The proprietor, assessing this customer's limited capacity, showed him the simplest *sidur,* but the man asked for something more elaborate. He continued asking for a more sophisticated *sidur* until the proprietor showed him the massive *Ozar Hatfilohs,* a *sidur* with hundreds of pages of scholarly commentaries on the prayers. The customer was overjoyed. This was exactly what he wanted.

The proprietor could not contain himself, "Why on earth would you want the *Ozar Hatfilohs*?" he asked, "Are you really able to understand this?" The customer shrugged. "Not at all", he said, "but you see, I have small children at home. When they get hold of a *sidur* and pretend to *daven,* they handle it so roughly that the first few pages are torn out. Now the *Adon Olam* (Master of the Universe) prayer is on the first page, and so they tear out the *Adon Olam.* With the *Ozar Hatfilohs,* there are so many pages of commentaries that even if they tear out many pages, they have a long way to go before they ever get to the *Adon Olam.*"

Father said, "The many customs and practices that were added to the Torah are there to assure that we keep the *Adon Olam* intact."

The term *Adon Olam* was cleverly exploited in this story. *Adon Olam* is, of course, the first prayer of the morning service, usually found on the first page of the *sidur*. Literally, however, *Adon Olam* means "Master of the Universe", and "tearing out the *Adon Olam*" means extirpating one's belief in God as ruler of the universe, that is, a rejection of faith in God.

There are many challenges to faith. It is abundantly clear that the world does not operate according to our logical understanding. Things constantly occur which lead people to question God's dominion and providence: "If there is a just God, why does He allow these things to happen?" If unfortunate happenings affect us more directly, and we experience suffering and distress, this question ceases to be a philosophical exercise and becomes a very angry challenge. At such times we need a great deal of reinforcement to maintain our faith.

It is also evident that the quality of faith has become attenuated with the progress of time. Each new generation is further removed from the revelation at Sinai. Father used to say that the difference between the Torah position of man's special creation by God and the evolutionary theory, is that according to the latter, man is constantly improving with each ensuing generation. Grandchildren are just a trifle more perfect and better developed than their grandparents since they have progressed two generations further from their simian ancestors. Little wonder that secularism has resulted in children thinking themselves to be wiser than their parents. According to Torah, however, we must realize that no matter how much greatness we have achieved or how learned we have become, each generation is nevertheless farther away from Adam, the direct handiwork of God. We must always aspire to reach the level of spirituality of earlier generations; we can never excel them.

It follows that with every ensuing generation we can anticipate an erosion of faith and the observances related to faith. How much our children will retain may well depend on what existed before the processes of erosion set in. If the lives of the parents are abundant in customs and traditions, the inevitable erosion may affect these, but not jeopardize the core of faith and commitment. Even if pages are torn away, they are the introductory pages; the *Adon Olam* remains intact. If, however, the parents have only the essential nucleus of faith, then the erosion process strikes this immediately. The very first deviation eliminates the *Adon Olam.*

◆§ §◆

Tradition was sacred all year round, but was eminently manifest on Passover, and rightly so. After all, this festival marked the occasion of the birth of our people, and was the beginning of our uniqueness.

Grandfather had lived in Belgium prior to World War II, and had escaped just ahead of the German occupation. Prior to his leaving Antwerp, he buried many of his Judaica, in the hope that they would one day be retrieved. After the war, they were indeed unearthed and sent to us.

Among the items was a beautiful spoon, gilt and decorated with artistic design. Father was overjoyed with this spoon, for it resurrected many childhood memories for him. It had been given as a gift to his grandfather.

Father used the spoon at the Seder, and then passed it around for us to use. I was thus in possession of a fourth-generation item! This was used by the great *zaddik* Rabbi Motele of Hornostipol, and it was a reminder of how I was tied to him. Prior to Father's death, he divided his few family treasures among the children. "I'd rather enjoy seeing you have them now than to think you will be arguing over them later," he said. He gave me the Seder spoon.

My children use the spoon at the Seder, as do their children. To the little ones, it is just a very unusual, ornate spoon. Before too long, though they will know that this spoon was used by their ancestor, Rebbe Motele of Hornostipol, and that this concrete item is evidence of the chain in which they are an important link. As sixth generation descendants of Rebbe Motele they will learn that Rebbe Motele came to be who he was, perhaps because he knew that he was the sixth generation descendant of the Baal Shem Tov. Just as that heritage stimulated him to greatness, so should their heritage serve as a stimulus for them.

For kids, Passover was all fun. Even the work was fun, carrying the all-year-round dishes down to the cellar, and bringing up the Passover utensils. But for the adults, preparation for Passover is a great deal of work. In fact, some say that just as all of the Seder ritual is to commemorate various incidents of the Exodus, so is the preparation for Passover in commemoration of the hard labor of the enslavement of our ancestors.

It is told that in the days of feudalism in Russia, some feudal lords got together for a drinking party. Although anti-Semitism prevailed widely, many of the nobelemen had their pet Jew who was a kind of mascot. As they imbibed, the conversation turned to their pet Jews, each describing the loyalty of their respective mascots.

"My Moshke," one lord said, "is completely devoted to me. He would do anything to please me. Why, if I told Moshke to jump into the fire, he wouldn't bat an eyelash."

"That's what you think," another responded. "Just tell your Moshke that you want him to defect from Judaism and convert to your religion, and he'll spit in your face."

Moshke's master downed another glass of vodka. "Never!" he protested. "Moshke does whatever I say. I'll show you."

Moshke was sent for, and he hurried to his master's bidding. "Moshke," the lord said, "You know how good I have been to you and have protected you all these years. Now, Moshke, why should we not worship the same God? Friends like us should not be separated by religions. Moshke, I want you to convert to my faith."

Moshke turned pale. "Your lordship," he said. "I will gladly give even my life for you. But a decision such as this I cannot make without the consent of my wife, for she too would have to convert. May it please your lordship, I will talk with my wife and come back shortly."

Moshe ran home breathlessly, "Bela!", he exclaimed. "We have *tzuris* (troubles). The *poritz* (lord) is *meschuge* (mad), and he wants me to convert to Christianity." Bela sat pensively. After a few minutes she said, "Look, Moshke. The *poritz* may be *meschuge,* but our lives are in his hands. If we defy him, we may be flogged or imprisoned, or both, or even killed. Moshke, God knows what is in our hearts. To satisfy the *poritz,* we can act as though we are Christians, but in our hearts we will still pray to our own God."

Moshke returned to the party with an affirmative answer. The triumphant lord proudly demonstrated to his colleagues the loyalty of his vassal, and called the priest to perform the conversion ritual.

Moshke and Bela began to attend mass and behave like devout Christians.

Two months passed, and the lord sent for Moshke. "Moshke," he said, "Do you think it really makes a difference to me what religion you practice? I only wished to test your loyalty and devotion to me, and you have well proven that. You can go back to being a Jew, Moshke."

Moshke ran home with the good tidings. "Bela!" he said, "We don't have to be *goyim* (Gentiles) any longer. We can go back to being Jews again, the *poritz* said. Isn't that wonderful!"

Bela was overjoyed, but after a moment took on a solemn

attitude. "Moshke," she said. It is three weeks until Passover. You now what kind of work that involves. Let's already remain *goyim* until Passover is over!"

❧

Sukkos (Feast of Tabernacles) is referred to as the "season of joy," and it was just that for me.

When I was a child, there were no pre-fabricated *sukkas* nor roof-coverings. Shortly before Sukkos, Chuna would come with a helper and get the lumber out of the garage for construction of the *sukka.* I would get the chance to use hammer and nails and all the wonderful tools.

Incidentally, one memory stands out in my mind. I had taken a long piece of lumber and hammered a nail into it for the fun of it. Chuna rebuked me saying, "Someone might try to saw that piece of wood, and when his saw is damaged on that nail, might curse the one who put that nail there. Never do things which might cause someone to curse you." A good point.

The greatest fun was going with Hersh on his horse and wagon to get willow branches for the covering of the *sukka.* I helped Hersh tie up the branches into bundles and load them onto the wagon. Today in my reveries, I can go back to those scenes, and sometimes even smell the freshly cut willows.

Today, *sukka* decorations can be purchased. In those days, we had to make our own. Father would do the lettering on cardboard, and we would fill in the colors. We painted the fruit with bronze paint to appear golden.

We made decorative birds for the *sukka*. Since there were no plastic balls, the body of the birds consisted of a hollow egg shell. This was fashioned by puncturing a raw egg at both ends and blowing out the contents. (This was the origin of the Yiddish expression that something is "as worthless as a blown-out egg.")

Wings were fashioned out of folded colored paper and attached to the egg shell with sealing wax. The bird's head was molded out of beeswax. This was a delicate process, and if the fragile egg shell was accidentally crushed, the whole procedure had to be repeated.

There were always many guests eating in our *sukka*, both intinerant rabbis and townspeople who had no *sukka* of their own. There was always singing and dancing, and the telling of many, many stories.

Simchas Torah marked the close of Sukkos. The joy of dancing with the Torahs knew no bounds. Whoever saw Father dance with the Torah has a memory never to be forgotten. Father's dance essentially defined the concept of joy as understood in chassidic teachings. Father would stand holding the Torah while joining in singing a joyous melody, a tune reserved exclusively for Simchas Torah, and one which our ancestor, the Maggid of Czernobl, had said that he had heard from the heavenly angels in their adoration of God. Father would then stand motionless while the singing continued, and then abruptly break into a dance which was at once serene yet ecstatic.

The message of the dance was that joy is an internal experience, and should find external expression only when it reaches an intensity at which it can no longer be contained. Then, and only then, may it burst out into spontaneous and manifest action. Even then, the expression of joy must be modest and subdued.

Years later when I learned chassidic elaborations on "rejoice with trembling" (Psalms II:11), I was able to understand them. Father's Simchas Torah dance was an indelible lesson.

❧

At Friday night services, Father would occasionally recite the mourner's *kaddish*. He told us the following story.

The Rebbe of Apt, an ancestor whose name (Abraham Joshua Heshel) I have the honor to bear, often lived in dire poverty. Some communities could not afford a salary for the rabbi, and the latter's livelihood consisted of the rabbi's wife having the exclusive rights to the sale of yeast. At the very best, this could provide a meager subsistence, but conditions were not often the very best.

One year the Sukkos festival approached with the Rebbe of Apt not having enough money to buy any food for the holiday, let alone candles, and certainly not enough to acquire an *esrog* and *lulav*. Not having anything to accomplish at home on the day preceding the holiday, the Rebbe returned to the synagogue early in the morning, cautioning his wife not to borrow any money nor accept any charity. Whatever the Almighty wished them to have, they would have.

After the Rebbe left, a stranger came to the door, and told the Rebetzin that he was a merchant en route home, and that he saw that he could not possibly reach his home before sundown. He therefore would have to spend *Yom Tov* in one of the towns on the way, and this was as good as any. However, since he was carrying a large sum of money with him, he wished to stay in a secure place, and the safest place he could think of was the home of the local rabbi. Therefore, could he please spend *Yom Tov* here?

The Rebetzin responded that they would certainly be pleased to have him at their home, but since they would be spending a hungry *Yom Tov*, it would hardly be appropriate to invite someone else to share their misery.

"That will be no problem," the stranger said, taking out a large bill from his purse. "It is early enough in the day to acquire provisions, and it is well worth the expense to be in a home where I can rest in peace and confidence."

The Rebetzin took the money and hurried to the market. The stranger, reasoning that the Rebbe certainly had no funds for an *esrog* and a *lulav*, went off to procure a set.

That night following services, the Rebbe tarried at the synagogue to continue his studies, knowing that there was nothing to rush home for, since he could fast at the synagogue just as well as at home. When he finally did return home, he was surprised to see from afar the glow of his *sukka*, since he knew that they had no candles. When he entered the *sukka* and saw the table set with *challos* and wine, his first thought was that the Rebetzin had not been able to make peace with having a barren *Yom Tov* and had succumbed to the temptation to accept alms. He therefore came into the house with a stern attitude, and rebuked his wife for going against his wishes.

"Heaven forbid!" the Rebetzin said, and then went on to tell him about the stranger that had asked for shelter, and had provided for the necessities for himself and them.

The Rebbe was beside himself with joy, for here the Almighty had provided him with the means for celebrating *Yom Tov* in a festive manner without his having to accept charity. When the stranger came in, the Rebbe embraced him, and when the latter showed the Rebbe the *esrog* and *lulav* with which he could fulfill the sacred *mitzvah*, the

Rebbe's elation knew no bounds. He took the stranger by the hands and danced with him into the *sukka*.

The Rebbe's face radiated with light as they sat down to the table, and the stranger took his place near the Rebbe. He was somewhat surprised when the Rebbe asked him to move down a bit, and then a bit farther, and so on until he was seated at the extreme end of the table. After the meal, the stranger approached the Rebbe. "Please do not misunderstand me," he said. "You really owe me nothing, since I bought the provisions primarily for my own need. Now if there were other guests in the *sukka*, I could understand that they perhaps deserved to sit closer to you than I do. But since you and I were the only ones in the *sukka*, why did you push me to the end of the table? Why did it bother you if I would sit near you?" he asked.

The Rebbe embraced the man. "My dear child," he said, "do not think that way. You are very precious to me, and only the Almighty can reward you for what you have done for me. But how can you say that there were no other guests in the *sukka*? You know that the Patriarchs, Abraham,Isaac, Jacob, Moses, Aaron, Joseph, and David visit the *sukka*. Where were they to sit? Please forgive me, but I had to make room for them."

The man's eyes widened and brightened. To think that he had the privilege of being in the company of the Patriarchs! He kissed the Rebbe's hands and embraced him. The following morning when they entered the *sukka*, the stranger immediately and joyfully took his place at the end of the table.

After the meal on the second night, the stranger approached the Rebbe. "Rebbe," he said, "if I have indeed been blessed with the privilege to share the *sukka* with the Patriarchs, I would like to actually see them."

The Rebbe shook his head. "No, my child," he said. "This would be a vision too intense for your soul to be contained within your body, and you have yet many years to live."

The following day, the stranger persisted. "I have given this much thought," he said. "I am already near sixty, and perhaps I may yet live ten or so years. I value the sight of the Patriarchs far more than a few years of earthly existence." The Rebbe tried to dissuade him, but as the stranger was adamant, he finally granted him the ability to behold the Patriarchs.

The following day the stranger took ill, and when the Rebbe sat at his bedside, he said, "I feel my energies leaving me, and I know I am going to die. Believe me, Rebbe, I have no regrets. The sight of the Patriarchs was worth a dozen years; I would gladly do it all over again. I have only one concern: I am childless. Who will say the *kaddish* for me?

The Rebbe assured the man that he would observe the *kaddish.* "But what about the *yahrzeit* (the annual memoriam)? You, too, are only mortal, and am I to be totally forgotten after your passing?"

The Rebbe thought a moment, and then said, "I will leave instructions in my will that my descendants shall recite the Friday night *kaddish* in your memory." Thus, father said the *kaddish* in memory of the stranger who had merited both the privilege of providing his ancestor with a festive *Yom Tov,* and also the privilege to see the ancestors of the Jewish nation.

Not all childhood memories are memories of fun. Some are quite solemn, but no less enjoyable.

Rosh Hoshanah and Yom Kippur were solemn days; solemn, yet festive.

In a sense, Rosh Hoshanah and Yom Kippur were anti-climactic. The preparationfor these several days had a greater impact on me than the days themselves.

Father hardly ever showed emotion during his prayer. His prayers were quiet and subdued. Having undergone surgery on his vocal cords, he never led the services, except for *Mincha* on the eve of Rosh Hoshanah, and *Ne'ilah* (the concluding service) on Yom Kippur.

Father's repetition of the *amidah* (the silent prayer) of *Mincha* on the eve of Rosh Hoshanah was soul-rending. The words were no different than the *amidah* which was said three times daily all year around. But this was the final *Amidah* of the year. It was one last opportunity to do a *mitzvah* in the remaining moments of the year about to end. If one had failed to have a proper attitude towards prayer and devotion during the entire year, here was one last chance.

"Return us, O Father, to Your Torah, and bring us back to serve You . . . forgive us our transgressions, for You are a forgiving King . . . heal us, and we shall be healed . . . return to Your sanctuary in Jerusalem . . ."

Every verse was saturated with tears, and the congregation wept along with him. Why had we not said these prayers this way all year? Why did we just mumble the words out of habit, and not grasp their full meaning? Never again will we allow these beautiful prayers to be said without feeling. Never!

After *Mincha,* I would hear some of the congregants say, "This year will certainly be a good one. The Rebbe has pleaded our cause well."

The day before Yom Kippur, at the morning meal, Father would sing the portion of the *Selichot* (prayer for forgiveness) services for that day. The melody penetrated every crevice in one's soul, and brought one to a profound state of atonement.

"How can I come before the Judge, without any merits in hand; and because of this, my heart is full of fear . . . To Your protective abode have come Your children whom You have exiled, and in Your house, they have gathered in fear and trembling." The tears poured forth profusely. "Remember for them the virtues of their ancestors as they stand in judgment before You . . ."

The Talmud states that it is a *mitzvah* to eat on the day before Yom Kippur. In fact, eating on that day is considered as though one would have fasted two consecutive days. The Talmud did not mean simply eating. It was referring to this morning meal when Father's rendition of the *Selichot* hymn dissected one's soul and achieved an even greater intensity of *tshuvah* (repentance) than Yom Kippur itself would accomplish.

Following this, Yom Kippur was anti-climactic, until the concluding service of the day, *Ne'ilah*. The fast was almost over, and everyone felt that they had merited Divine forgiveness. Then Father chanted the prayer of the thirteen Divine attributes of mercy, the prayer vouchsafed by God to Moses with the promise that it will never be turned away.

It suddenly hit us. What if we have not repented sincerely? What if we have not merited forgiveness? What if we have allowed this precious day of forgiveness to slip by without achieving true *tshuvah*? And now we were in the very last few moments of this day. But all was not lost. There was still this one and final opportunity to avail ourselves of the Divine forgiveness of the day.

"I place my entire trust in these thirteen words, and in the gates of tears which are never closed; and thusly I pour out my heart before the Searcher of all hearts . . ." Father's voice was now barely audible as it broke through his tears. "May it be Your will, He who hears the supplication of those who weep, that You preserve our tears with you, and spare us from all evil, for to You and only to You do we suspend our eyes in trust and hope . . ."

After *N'eilah* everyone felt that a heavy burden had been lifted from their hearts. Instantaneously, the mood changed from one of deep concern to exultation.

Immediately after the close of the day, Father would telephone family members who lived elsewhere to wish them, "May your prayers have been accepted," and to inquire as to how they had tolerated the fast.

Father reflected the chassidic disenchantment with non-compulsory fasting, often quoting the great Rebbe of Karlin. "If only I had the authority," said the Rebbe of Karlin, "I would do away with all fasting except for *Tisha B'av,* for who *can* eat on the day commemorating the destruction of the sanctuary and Yom Kippur, for who even *cares* about eating?

The dislike of fasting was due to the fact that after one has fasted, and has felt the hunger and discomfort of the fast, one is subject to feel that he has indeed made a great sacrifice for God, and now truly merits Divine favor. Fasting may thus lead to the loss of humility, and this is too great a risk to be taken.

The great Maggid said, "Fasting makes a small defect in the body, but when you create a small defect in the body, you can create a large defect in the soul." Better to eat and plan to use the energy wisely in the service of God, than to fast and to think that you have thereby already achieved saintliness.

❧

Before Yom Kippur, there is a traditional ritual of "kapporos," or "exchange." Essentially, the person seeking forgiveness is given to understand that in his defying Divine will by committing transgressions, he has forfeited his right to life. However, he is permitted to offer an "exchange" for his life by having a chicken slaughtered in his stead. The apparent rationale for this is that rather than the concept of capital punishment being a total abstraction, the penitent sees his penalty carried out in actuality on a lower form of life, and this should help him recognize the gravity of his transgression. The chicken is then given away to the needy.

One of the disciples of Rebbe Elimelich came to the Master before Yom Kippur, asking for a more profound understanding of the '"kapporos" ritual. "I cannot help you," Rebbe Elimelich said, "but if you will go to the inn in the nearby village, the innkeeper may be able to instruct you in the concept of 'exchange.' "

The disciple promptly left for the specified inn, and upon arriving, was taken aback by the appearance of the innkeeper. He had assumed that the Rebbe had sent him to a pious man of great learning, but what he found was a quite uncouth, ignorant person, who was serving drinks to his customers and indulging in idle gossip with them.

"Certainly this man must be one of the secret *zaddikim*, masquerading as an ignorant, unrefined person," the disciple thought. Yet in watching the innkeeper's behavior, he could find no redeeming features nor any trace of acts of devotion to God.

That night, after all the customers had left and the inn was closed, the innkeeper asked his wife to bring him a huge ledger. He opened the book, and began to read off all of the transgressions he had committed during the past year. From time to time he would pause, heave a sigh of distress, shake his head in remorse, and go on with the litany.

After completing the long list of transgressions, he asked his wife for a second huge ledger. From this one, he began to read all of the misfortunes that God had visited upon him during the past year."Here is one where I bought a cask of wine, and it turned sour on me; and I lost a great deal of money. Then there was the storm that tore the roof off my house. Here a step went out from under me, and I fell and broke my arm." And so on, and so on, until he completed a long list of grievances against God.

The innkeeper then put both ledgers together and turned his eyes upward. "Listen, *Ribono Shel Olam* (Master of the Universe), I know I have not done right by You, but on the other hand, You have really not done right by me either. Since we are approaching the day of forgiveness, let us make an even exchange. I will forgive You, You will forgive me, and we will begin the new year with a clean slate."

The disciple returned to Rebbe Elimelich with the account of this unusual exchange. "That is the true spirit of 'kaporos,' " the Rebbe said. "Forgiveness must be universal. Man must learn to forgive his fellow man, and man must also learn not to carry a grudge against the Almighty when misery befalls him. This simple man was most sincere. He recognized that he had committed wrongs, and knew that his sufferings had not been purposeless, but rather considered them to be punishments which he had deserved. In forgiving God for what He had done to him, he asserted his faith in Divine Providence, and that is the ultimate of man's existence."

Little wonder that the Baal Shem Tov held the simple folk in such high esteem. The sincerity of their faith was unequalled.

❧

What is *Shabbos*? Why, a day of rest, of course.

This is only partially true. Many people take a day of rest in order to restore their energies and recharge their batteries for the days ahead. The day of rest is thus a means, a preparation for something else.

Shabbos is not a day of rest in this sense. Quite the contrary, *Shabbos* is the ultimate goal rather than a means to some other end. *Shabbos* is not a preparation for the week to come. Rather, the work week is a preparation for *Shabbos*.

This is clearly stated in the inaugural prayer on Friday night. "You have sanctified the seventh day, the completion and goal of the work of creation."

Shabbos is a day of study, of reflection, of prayer, of people getting closer to one another, of families being together. So many things are restricted on *Shabbos* that there is nothing left but involvement in the above. Thus, *Shabbos* brings man closer to God and to his fellow man, and that is the purpose of creation.

In our home, as in many others, if one spoke on *Shabbos* about anything that was going to occur after *Shabbos*, it had to be prefaced with *"nisht um Shabbos geredt"* (not to be spoken of on *Shabbos*) as a reminder that although one might talk of post-*Shabbos* events, one should not do any planning on *Shabbos*.

The *halacha* is unusually harsh with one who knowingly and intentionally violates *Shabbos*. Little wonder, *Shabbos* is what Jewishness is all about.

⁂

The very beauty and euphoria of *Shabbos* is responsible for the let-down or "after-*Shabbos* blues" that often occurs at the close of *Shabbos*.

Father helped assuage this by reciting in Yiddish the prayer of Rebbe Levi Yitzchok of Berdichev before *Havdalah* (the closing ceremony of *Shabbos*). "God of Abraham, of Isaac and of Jacob, protect Your people Israel from all evil. The holy *Shabbos* is departing, and may this week come to us with good health, *mazel*, blessing, success, wealth, honor *nachas*, reverence of God, and all that is good." Father recited this three times to a pleasant melody that will stay with me forever.

Then the *Havdalah* proper began, composed of excerpts from the Scriptures. "Behold, God is my salvation; I trust in Him and I have no fear . . . the God of hosts is with us, the God of Jacob is our fortress. God of hosts, how fortunate is the person who has trust in You . . . And for the Jews there was light and joy and gladness and honor; so may it be for us."

The genius of Yiddishkeit counteracted the blues with the *Shabbos* night meal or *Melave Malke* (lit., escorting the *Shabbos* Queen).

The menu of the *Melave Malke* was usually standard:

herring, cooked potatoes, and tea or coffee. Its stimulating effect derived not from culinary delight, but from the stories. Whereas during the *Shabbos* meals Father would expound on the weekly portion of the Torah, *Melave Malke* was for stories of the great *zaddikim*.

I feel fortunate in that I heard many stories about *zaddikim* from eyewitnesses. I knew many people who were *chassidim* of my great-grandfather, Rebbe Motele. I knew several people who had looked into the eyes of the Zeide of Sanz. Grandfather knew the Zeide of Cherkassy, who studied two years under the great Rebbe Shneur Zalman, author of the Tanya. With two or three intermediates, I was in contact with the great Maggid of Mezeritch and his many disciples, and with the Baal Shem Tov himself.

I began absorbing these stories while in my cradle. There were accounts of the wondrous deeds of the great *zaddikim,* some no less miraculous than the splitting of the Red Sea by Moses. There were stories that depicted the characters of the great *zaddikim.* Although there were no authentic pictures of them, I could imagine what the Zeide of Sanz looked like, or Rebbe Zusia, or the Zeide of Shpole. However, I never could conjure up an image of the Baal Shem Tov, and I always wondered why he escaped my childhood imaginative skills. Many years later I read that one of the Baal Shem Tov's disciples upon meeting Rebbe Heshel, the Baal Shem Tov's son, remarked that he was thrilled to see him. "When I think of the greatness of the Master," he said, "I find it difficult to believe that he was a human being. I think that he was an angel who was but disguised as a human, just as were the angels who visited the Patriarch Abraham. But now that I see you, I am reassured that he was indeed a human being." Perhaps the rather weak ties the Baal Shem Tov had with his physical being precluded my conjuring up an image of the person.

Were all the stories we heard true? Father would often say that anyone who believes all the stories about the *zaddikim* to be factual is credulous, but that anyone who denies their possibility of being true was a heretic.

Father used to say that there is a tradition that telling a story about the Baal Shem Tov at *Melave Malke* is conducive to *parnassa* (financial success). He said that there were three errors in this tradition: 1) Not only a story about the Baal Shem Tov, but about any *zaddik;* 2) Not only at *Melave Malke* but at any time; 3) Not only conducive to *parnassa,* but to every desirable goal.

Along with the inspiring stories of the great *zaddikim* were stories about chassidim, or about the sincerity of the simple folk, which were no less inspiring. And these were not legends of ancient times. I looked into the eyes that looked into the eyes of one who was a disciple of Rebbe Shneur Zalman. Not only were these people real to me, but close enough that I felt it was not beyond possibility to emulate them.

There were stories of how the great *zaddikim* considered the entire world to be one great school, and that everything they saw was a personal teaching for them. Rebbe Moshe Leib of Sasov was once very discouraged at his failure to redeem a Jew who had been thrown into debtor's prison by his feudal master. On the way home he encountered a thief who had just been freed from imprisonment, and who was reprimanded, "Now after this punishment you will know never to steal again." The thief shrugged. "Who knows," he said, "maybe next time I will be luckier." Rebbe Moshe Leib felt that this was a teaching directed to him. Just because you fail once doesn't mean you don't try again. The great men learned from everyone, even from thieves.

One of the *zaddikim* was on his way home from the house of study late one night when he passed a tailor's shop. The tailor, weary from a day's work, was about to put down the garment he was sewing, when his wife remarked, "Better finish the work while the candle still burns. Soon it will flicker and go out."

The *zaddik* turned about and went back to the house of study. He had heard the message. Finish the work while the light of your soul still glows. Soon it may flicker and go out.

Father used to tell how the great Rebbe Shalom of Belz in eulogizing his wife related that she would awaken him at the break of dawn, saying, "The farmers and the tailors have already arisen to their work. Shalom, Shalom, it is time that you arise to your duties."

We would hear stories that stressed the primacy of sincere devotion. One Rosh Hashanah Rabbi Levi Yitzchok of Berdichev did not allow his congregation to begin services. "In a nearby field," he told the worshippers, "there is a young shepherd who was orphaned as a child, and did not get any schooling. He has never learned how to read. When he saw all the townsfolk going to *shul,* he was brokenhearted because he did not know how to *daven* . He turned his eyes to heaven and said, Almighty God, You know that I wish to praise You but I do not know how to read the prayers. So I will recite the letters, and You put them together to make the right words. Aleph, Beth, Gimmel, Daled. . ..

"And so" continued Rabbi Levi Yitzchok, "we must delay our *davening* a bit, because God is now busy putting together the letters for the shepherd."

Or I would hear of Rebbe Refael of Bershid who said, "We must give thanks to God that He made humility a *mitzvah*, and conceit an *avera* (sin) for what would I have done had God decreed that conceit was a *mitzvah*? How could I ever have fulfilled that *mitzvah*? What do I have that I could possibly be conceited about?"

Or I heard about Rebbe Shmelke of Nikolsburg who once came to a community where a large throng of his admirers welcomed him. Before greeting the crowd he asked for a few moments of privacy. Someone listened at the door of the room where he had secluded himself and heard him saying to himself, "Welcome, Rebbe! We are so fortunate to have you here . . . Oh great *zaddik*, give me a *bracha* (blessing). . . Holy Rebbe, you are the greatest *zaddik*. . ." and so on, heaping grandiose praises upon himself.

Later Rebbe Shmelke explained, "I know how my followers get carried away with their adoration, and just in case my head might be turned by some of their remarks, I said these all to myself first. They sounded so empty and ridiculous, that when I later heard the same words from them, they no longer made any impression."

These anecdotes of the great, as well as stories of their marvelous deeds, flowed copiously at *Melave Malke*. What an uplifting way to begin a new week with a renewal of faith, accompanied by a sense of challenge and the security that nothing can stand in the way of closeness to God as long as one is sincere.

Lebedig, Kinderlach! You have good reason to be joyful and merry. You are never more than seventy-two hours away from a *Shabbos*, the great *Shabbos* that was, or the one that will be.

Although *Shabbos* was a frequent celebration, it never

became boring, and never lost its uniqueness.

Even as a child, I do not recall envying other children whose activities were unrestricted, because they could listen to the radio, go to movies and ball games, go for rides, or do any of the many things which were prohibited for me.

By noon Friday, the aroma of the gefilte fish and the fresh *challa* filled the house. Friday night we partook of these delicacies as well as a peppered *lokshen kugel. Shabbos* morning, I awoke to the aroma of the *cholent,* which permeated the house. *Kiddush* on Shabbos morning was graced by two *kugels* which mother made weekly: a *lokshen kugel* and a sweet *kugel.* There is probably no more potent sedative than *cholent* plus *kugel* plus *kiddush* wine plus eggs with onion or chopped liver, and this often resulted in an afternoon nap. Although some toys and games were not permitted, we played word games galore or went for long hikes.

As a child, I could not understand, what do people who do not observe *Shabbos* do for pleasure? I am now much older and have seen a great deal of the world. I still ask the same question.

VII

Prayer

Although I had read much about the intensity and fervor of prayer, and although I had observed many pious people in devout prayer, this was not translated from the abstract to the concrete until an experience in Jerusalem at the *kotel*, our beautiful wall, that indestructable remnant of the Sanctuary, of which the Talmud states, "Never has the Divine Presence moved from the Western Wall." To stand at the *kotel* today is to have the closest approximation to God which a human is permitted in his earthly existence.

A man was being escorted to the *kotel*, obviously a blind man, guided by others on either side. He was a Sephardic Jew, his sharp, graceful features accentuated by thin, curly earlocks. He approached the *kotel*, and leaned forward to give it an affectionate kiss. He ran his hands over its surface, his super-sensitive fingers feeling centuries of history, glory, and suffering in every crevice and ripple. Then he began his dialogue with God. Yes, a dialogue, for although only one voice was audible, he knew that he had a responsive listener.

He spoke directly, respectfully and with great clarity, exactly as if the conversation were with a person. He gestured with his hands to provide the necessary emphasis and description that his words required. At one point, he abruptly stopped, hesitated a moment and said, "Oh, I'm sorry. I already told You that yesterday."

This was simple and sincere prayer at its best. There was no doubt in this man's mind that what he had told God yesterday was heard, and that there was therefore no reason to repeat it.

I turned back to continue reciting the Psalms, realizing that I had never really prayed before.

Our great-grandfather, the Rebbe of Hornostipol, was asked by a chassid, "Why is it that my prayers go unanswered? Were we not assured that God would grant the wishes of those who do His will? Why is it that the prayers of a *zaddik* are more effective than the prayers of an average person?"

The Rebbe replied, "A person's sincere wish is never denied, but that wish must be the person's foremost desire, and very few people pray for what is truly their foremost desire.

"Take, for example, the person who prays for success and wealth. He may indeed be impoverished and may very profoundly desire to become wealthy. Yet, if he were drowning and could not catch his breath, he would, of course, not think of acquiring wealth. At that point, his most fervent and only desire would be to breathe and remain alive, hence wealth is not really his first priority.

"The Talmud states that if a person forgoes his own needs

to pray for the needs of another, that prayer is warmly received.

"The devotion of a *zaddik* to his followers is so great," the Rebbe continued, "that their well-being becomes his first priority. The love of the *zaddik* for his fellow Jew surpasses the love and devotion of a father for his favorite child. When a *zaddik* prays for someone's health and success, his desire for that person's happiness is so intense, that even if the *zaddik* were drowning at that point, his prayer would not be for his own survival, nor his wish to be able to breathe and remain alive, but rather that the other person's needs be fulfilled. This self-negation and self-sacrifice which the *zaddik* achieves out of love for his fellow man is the reason why his prayers are answered."

The Rebbe knew of what he spoke. It is told that as a child, orphaned at a tender age, he was reared by his grandfather, the *zaddik* of Cherkassy. Once one of the Rebbe's adherents came to Cherkassy to beg the Rebbe to pray for his salvation. He had not earned enough to meet the payments on the inn and dwelling which he was renting from the feudal lord, and the latter had threatened him with expulsion and imprisonment if his arrears were not promptly resolved. He could see no source of help, and asked the Rebbe to pray for Divine mercy, so that he and his family would not languish in prison.

To his horror, he found that the Rebbe was out of the city, and when he approached the Rebetzin with his bitter plight, she suggested, "Go to the house of study and talk to my grandson. He may be able to help you."

"But your grandson is only a child of ten," the man said. "I need the Rebbe. Our very lives are in jeopardy."

Again the Rebetzin said, "The Rebbe is not available now.

Go talk with my grandson."

The man went to the house of study, where the ten-year-old child was engrossed in Talmud studies, and against his better judgment, unburdened himself to the young boy. The young boy listened sympathetically to the man's tearful tale of woe, sighed deeply, and said, "If only Grandfather were here, I am certain that he could help you. But there is nothing I can do for you."

In desperation, the man cried out, "Look, your grandmother sent me to you. Now, if you truly cannot help me, then I hold no grudge against you. But if you have the capacity to help me and refrain from doing so, then I shall never forgive you for what will befall my family. Not only will I not forgive you in this world, but I will not forgive you in the eternal word as well."

The young boy was shaken. He slowly closed the volume of the Talmud and said, "Well, let us go first to the *mikva*."

The man accompanied the young boy to the *mikva* and stood by as the latter immersed himself beneath the surface of the water. After a few moments, the man become concerned that the child was not coming out of the water, and as the moments passed, far beyond what seemed to be the human endurance for surviving without air, the man became panic-stricken. He tried to go down to the *mikva* to extricate the child, but his limbs seemed to be paralyzed. He soon forgot about his troubles, about his being in arrears, and about his imminent eviction or imprisonment. He was totally occupied with the child whose head remained immersed beneath the water. "Dear God," he prayed silently and fervently, "just let me see that young child emerge from the *mikva* alive."

After what seemed to be not one but many eternities, the

young boy emerged from the water. "Go home," he said. "You have nothing to worry about."

Several weeks later, the chassid returned to the Rebbe of Cherkassy and told him that upon his return home, the feudal lord had sent for him and apologized to him for having been so harsh with him. That previous night, the feudal lord related, he developed a choking sensation and was unable to breathe.In his panic he began to reflect that perhaps he was being punished by God for being so ruthless with his tenants. He then resolved that henceforth he would be more lenient with them, and soon thereafter his breathing returned to normal. "So," he said, "I will not only forgive you your arrears but I will also arrange more liberal terms for your future payments."

The Rebbe of Cherkassy shook his head sadly, "This is too tender an age for him to place his life in jeopardy." But the pattern that was inititated at age ten persisted for the next fifty-three years. The wants and needs of others took priority, always.

ঌ ঌ

Do we really know what to pray for?

Mother, who had gone through a great deal of suffering in her life, used to comment that she doubts that the *kalah* and the *choson* (bride and groom) at their wedding know how to exploit their special moment of grace. Tradition has it that for the couple the wedding day is their Yom Kippur, a day of total forgiveness of their past transgressions, and an opportunity to begin a new life without a blemish. They are thus in an unusual state of grace, and their prayers are more readily received with Divine favor.

"I wonder," she would say. "Do these two young children know how to exploit this precious opportunity? Do they anticipate the many problems that lie ahead, and the difficulties in raising their children? Being so young, inexperienced, and naive, not knowing what awaits them, they hardly know what to pray for." Then she would quote Shaw, "Youth is so precious. What a pity it is wasted on children."

When one of our children took his first steps, and we would call home with the good news, Mother would say, "Mazel Tov! God grant that he always walk in good paths."

Then Mother would relate that when I began walking, there was an itinerant rabbi guesting at our home, whose lot in life it was to go from door to door soliciting money, a practice which had earned him the uncomplimentary appellation of "*schnorrer*" (moocher).

Mother related that when I took my first steps, everyone in the room clapped their hands and shouted with glee, "Mazel Tov! *Dos kind geht.* " (The child is walking.)

The rabbi sadly shook his head. "When I began walking," he said, "my parents rejoiced, too. Everybody happily shouted, '*Dos kind geht.*' But today, nobody is happy when I walk into their homes. *Vi ich geh, vill men mich nisht.*" (Wherever I go, people do not want me.)

Then Mother would say, "When a child starts walking, the parents should pray that God grant that just as his walking is so welcomed now, his life should be such that *Vi er geht zoll men zich frehen mit ihm.*" (Wherever he goes, people should be happy to see him.)

Do most of us really know what to pray for?

Our Grandfather of Sanz used to relate this parable before Rosh Hoshanah.

A king had to punish his wayward son by banishing him to a distant land. The prince, who had never learned any trade, was at a loss as to how to support himself, and wandered from village to village, looking for something which he might be able to do to earn a livelihood.

He finally chose to become a shepherd, since this required no particular skill. But he found this work unbearable, because he was exposed for many hours to the hot sun in the wide-open pastures.

The prince noted that other shepherds would build themselves little huts of sticks and branches, but try as he might, he could never construct a hut for himself. Never having learned to do any manual labor, every attempt to construct a hut resulted in failure. Thus the months and years went by, with the prince suffering the discomfort of the scorching sun.

One day the prince learned from the villagers that a great and rare event was soon to take place. The king was coming to visit a nearby city, and there would be a grand parade, to which people would flock from all the nearby villages. There was a tradition that anyone could write a request on a slip of paper, and as the royal coach passed, could try to throw it into the coach. The king would read those petitions that landed in the coach, and grant the particular requests.

On the day of the parade, the prince joined the villagers going to the city. Writing on a slip of paper, he requested that he be given a little hut that he could take with him to the pasture to protect him from the heat of the sun. As the royal coach passed, he threw his petition, which fell at the feet of the king.

As the king opened the little note, he immediately recognized his son's handwriting, and began to weep bitterly. "How deeply my child has deteriorated," he cried. "He no longer recalls that he is a prince. He does not ask to return to the royal court where he would lack nothing. His highest aspiration is to have a little hut, to be less uncomfortable in the lowly position to which he has resigned himself."

Grandfather wept along with the king in the parable. "On Rosh Hoshanah," he said, "we are given access to the Divine King, to present our petitions. This one asks for wealth, this one asks for relief from some oppressors, this one asks for recovery from an illness, and this one asks for a more comfortable dwelling. They have forgotten that they are princes. They do not ask to be permitted to return home from exile, where in the royal court all their needs would be satisfied. How deeply hurt our Father must be when he receives our petitions, and sees that we have forgotten our unique relationship to Him, and have resigned ourselves to a lowly status, where our aspirations are not higher than the equivalent of a thatched hut."

No, many of us really do not know how to pray.

⁂

Torah teachings are replete with the concept of man's personal relationship to God, and God's interest in every living being. The Jew prays to God several times each day, and although he may be bewildered why God is not answering his prayers by fulfilling his requests, he nevertheless knows he is being heard.

Many people are frustrated when their prayers seem to be unanswered. They seem to confuse prayer with command. It is as though God is supposed to obey and fulfill their every wish. In essence, they have matters reversed, and seem to believe they are God's master instead of the other way around.

There is a lovely story of a little girl who came crying to her mother because her doll's arm came off. The mother, who was very busy with her housework and did not know what to do, replied, "Well, go pray to God and ask Him to fix it."

A bit later, the mother was surprised to observe that the child was playing happily. "Is your dolly's arm all better?" she asked. "Did God take care of it?"

The child replied, "I asked Him to fix it but He said, 'No.' "

The child had a better understanding of prayer than the mother, and for that matter, than most of us. Not everything we ask for is granted. God may say, "No," but that doesn't mean that He wasn't listening.

During the lifetime of the great chassidic master, the Maggid of Mezeritch, there were no evil decrees against Jews, an unusual phenomenon in the bitterly anti-Semitic czarist Russia. After the Maggid's death, however, the decrees recurred. Many of the Maggid's disciples were perplexed, for the Talmud says that the righteous have greater powers in heaven after their death than during their lifetime on earth. How is it then that during his lifetime the Maggid was able to ward off evil decrees with his prayers, but was no longer able to do so after his death?

The Maggid appeared in a dream to one of his disciples and said, "You must know that God never does evil, but there are things which human perception interprets as evil, even though they are ultimately good. It is much like an unsophisticated person observing surgery. Not knowing anything about disease and healing, he may think that cutting open a human being is the height of torture and cruelty. One who understands realizes that the surgeon is doing something essential for the person's survival.

"When I lived on earth," the Maggid said, "and with my human eyes I perceived a given decree to be evil, I prayed to God to annul it. Now that I am in a higher world, where I am permitted to see the ultimate good in everything, I cannot intercede to revoke that which is good. If you on earth perceive it as evil, then *you* should pray for its revocation."

❧

The ultimate test of faith is the acceptance of adversity. There is little challenge when things go well, but to trust in Divine providence when one is a victim of suffering, when one feels that a benevolent Father would have protected one from distress, that is the acid test of faith.

When the *Shema* (affirmation of faith: Hear O Israel, the Lord thy God, the Lord is One) is recited, it is customary to put the hands over the eyes as a covering. Father explained that this was a symbolic gesture, indicating that although our sense perceptions may tell us that what we are experiencing is bad, we are willing to let our faith supercede and overrule our perception. We affirm that God is one and is always merciful, but since our own perceptions may conflict with this, we therefore cover our eyes as an assertion that our perceptions and judgment may be incorrect, and that the ultimate truth and goodness rest with the infinite wisdom and judgment of God.

We recite the *Shema* upon arising to help us confront the happenings of the day with the conviction that all will be for the good, and again upon retiring at night to reaffirm our faith in the benevolence of Divine wisdom.

Even that which we may see as distressful is in reality good. *Lebedig, kinderlach, lebedig.*

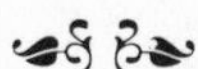

VIII

Tzdaka

The importance and greatness of the *mitzvah* of *tzdaka* has been emphasized and re-emphasized in Jewish *halacha* and lore since Sinai. Yet I doubt that it had ever reached its pinnacle until it was exercised by the Rebbe of Sanz.

The Rebbe of Sanz was a rather recent ancestor of ours. Inasmuch as Father and Mother were both descendants of the Rebbe of Sanz, we heard many stories on both sides of the family about the *tzdaka* of the Sanzer Zeide.

The Sanzer Zeide had legions of followers, and they would give him donations amounting to vast sums of money. But everything he received was promptly given away to the poor as *tzdaka*.

It should be remembered that in Galicia there was no welfare system. The poor were poor, and there were no resources to mitigate their poverty. The poor needed not only food, clothing, and shelter, but also help with tuition for their children, medical care, funds to try and start a business which could extricate them from poverty, and money to provide for the needs of children who were to be married.

The Sanzer Zeide never went to sleep if there was even a single coin left in the house. Everything had to be given away to the poor. When he was told that the wealthy have strong-boxes in which they keep their money, he responded in wonderment, "How can they sleep at night?"

Grandmother once took him severely to task for his lavish *tzdaka.* She had been at the marketplace, and was unable to buy a duck because it was too expensive. "Do you know who *did* buy the duck?" she asked. "It was that woman who comes to you every week for charity. She is so destitute, yet spends her money on delicacies."

The Zeide responded, "Is that so? I am so grateful that you told me. I did not know that she needed to buy duck. Now I will make certain to give her additional money so that she can afford to buy duck."

Anything of value in the house was pawned, and the money given away. Zeide's chassidim would redeem his silver *Kiddush* cup from the pawn shop on Fridays. In case they missed doing so, he would recite the *Kiddush* using a plain glass. Similarly, the Chanukah menorah was pawned all year round.

The Zeide's eldest son once reminded him that *halacha* dictates that one should not give more than twenty per cent of one's assets to *tzdaka.* The Zeide's reaction was painful. "Who has ever heard of a child being so cruel to his own father!" he cried. "Woe is me, that I have lived to see my child having no mercy on me.

"I am not giving *tzdaka* as a *mitzvah,*" the Zeide said. "I am giving *tzdaka* as an atonement for my many sins. Any person would give away everything he owns to redeem his very life. There is no limit in *halacha* as to how much you may spend to save your own life.

"What value does my learning have? What value does my *davening* have? Of what value are all my *mitzvohs* which I perform so imperfectly? But *tzdaka* does not require perfection in its performance to be of merit. If the poor have what to eat and with what to clothe themselves, then the *tzdaka* is meritorious. The only *mitzvah* I can perform adequately in my sad state of sinfulness is *tzdaka*, and my own child begrudges this of me."

One time the Zeide gave a sizable sum to a vulgar rogue. The chassidim were beside themselves, and asked the Zeide why he gave *tzdaka* to such an undeserving person.

"Let me tell you a story of Rebbe Zusia," the Zeide said. "Rebbe Zusia had a chassid who would from time to time give him some funds to support himself. This chassid achieved considerable success in his business. One time he found out that Rebbe Zusia had gone to Mezeritch to his master, the great Maggid. The chassid then reasoned, 'If the Maggid is Rebbe Zusia's master, he must obviously be an even greater *zaddik* than Rebbe Zusia himself,' and he then discontinued visiting Rebbe Zusia, and became a devotee of the great Maggid.

"From that day on, his business began to fail, and continued on a downhill course. The chassid then returned to Rebbe Zusia and said, 'I recognize that this is not a coincidence, but I do not understand why my fortunes took a turn for the worse when I began to be a follower of your Rebbe, who you must admit is even greater than you.'

"Reb Zusia responded, 'You see, my son, the Almighty deals with us according to how we deal with others. As long as you would help support someone as undeserving as Zusia, the Almighty was bountiful to you, whether or not you were deserving of reward. But when you began to be selective and gave your support only to the great *zaddikim*, then the Almighty reacted by becoming more selective in choosing the recipients of His bounty.' "

The Sanzer Zeide then said, "As long as I am not selective as to whom I give *tzdaka*, then I can hope that the Almighty will be merciful and bountiful even to someone as lowly and undeserving as me. But if I will start being selective and give only to those who are truly deserving, with what right can I ask the Almighty for anything for myself?"

Mother's father, the Rebbe of Bobov, used to say, "The Zeide is generally considered to have been a genius in Talmud and a *zaddik* in his *tzdaka*. It is not appreciated that he was also a genius in *tzdaka* as well." He cited the following story.

Before Sukkos, the Zeide's *tzdaka* intensified, if that were possible. He did not permit decorations in his *sukka*. "Gifts to the poor are ornaments for the *sukka*," he would say. Not only did he give away everything he owned, as was his usual custom, but he also borrowed heavily to give *tzdaka* and to make sure that the poor would be able to celebrate the festive holiday with joy.

One Sukkos, only minutes before sunset and the beginning of the holiday, a messenger came to one of the more wealthy people in Sanz, stating that the Rebbe requested an immediate loan of a rather sizable sum. The man promptly sent the requested money, but his curiosity was aroused. He knew that in the past few days, the Rebbe had already disbursed an enormous amount of money to all of the poor in town. Furthermore, it was now so late in the day that the recipient of the money could not possibly put it to use for *Yom Tov* anyway. What would the Rebbe do with this money?

The man therefore followed the messenger and noted that the money was delivered to a family for whose *Yom Tov* needs the Rebbe had already amply provided. He then proceeded to ask the Rebbe why this extra gift was necessary.

The Sanzer Zeide responded, "You are going to teach me how to give *tzdaka*? Here, let me teach you something.

"Yes," he said, "I did give this family enough for adequate provisions for *Yom Tov*. But the head of this family is deeply in debt. How is he going to enjoy the *Yom Tov* when he knows that immediately after *Yom Tov* he will be hounded by his creditors? Does not the Torah say that one must rejoice on *Yom Tov*? Is food and drink sufficient to provide joy? Is it not my responsibility to enable the family to have *simcha* on *Yom Tov*? But now that he has some money in reserve and knows that immediately after *Yom Tov* he will be able to make payments on his debts, he and his family will be able to share in the joy of *Yom Tov*."

The Zeide was truly a genius in *tzdaka*.

❧

We all perform charitable acts, but even in doing so, we must not let our emotions cloud our rational thoughts.

Rebbe Zusia's wife one time pressed him for money to make herself a new dress.

"I'm simply ashamed to go among people in rags," she said. And when Rebbe Zusia's wife said "rags," she was not using the term colloquially to refer to a perfectly good garment which had merely gone out of style. She meant a threadbare garment with multiple patches.

Rebbe Zusia could not resist her entreaties. He found

someone who was willing to lend him money, and his wife bought material for a dress.

For a while, there was peace and happiness in Rebbe Zusia's home. One day, however, Rebbe Zusia noticed that his wife was dejected. He asked her for the cause of her misery.

"I went to the tailor to get my dress," she said, "and when he handed it to me he sighed deeply, and his eyes welled up with tears. I asked him why he was so depressed, and he told me that he is marrying off a daughter in a few weeks. He was quite poor, all of his meager earnings having gone to feed his large family. He could not afford a wedding dress for his daughter, and she had been very sad about this."

"One day the daughter walked into the shop, and she saw her father completing the work on my dress. She jumped to the conclusion that this was to be her wedding dress with which her father was going to surprise her. She asked to try on the dress, and it fit her perfectly. She was ecstatic with joy, until her father told her that the dress was not for her, but was made for a customer. The tailor told me that the girl became very depressed, and is now talking about not wanting to get married, and wishes to break the engagement.

"I could not stand to see the tailor's pain," Rebbe Zusia's wife continued, "so I told the tailor to give the dress to his daughter. After all, you won't divorce me if I don't have a new dress, and as far as the townfolk are concerned, they are quite accustomed to see me in *shmatas* (rags)."

Rebbe Zusia was overjoyed with his wife's act of kindness. "Thank God you were able to overcome your personal desires, my dear wife," he said. "You have done one of the greatest *mitzvohs* possible. But tell me, did you pay the tailor for his work?"

"Pay him?" Rebbe Zusia's wife exclaimed "I should pay him? Isn't it enough that I gave away the dress I have been waiting for so long, should I pay him yet?"

Rebbe Zusia responded, "I am certain that the tailor counted on this wage to support his family. You contracted for a dress, and he did his work admirably, just as you had requested. You owe him the money for his work. The fact that you were moved to do an act of kindness and gave him the dress for his daughter does not absolve you from your obligation to pay him for his work. Business is business, and *tzdaka* is *tzdaka.*"

Rebbe Zusia borrowed additional money, and made his wife pay the tailor.

❧

A man once came to the home of Rebbe Zusia, asking for alms. Rebbe Zusia, being indigent himself, had nothing to give the man, and was terribly upset over this. He searched the house for something of value which he might give him, and he found, tucked away in the drawer, the headpiece which his wife had worn at their wedding. There were several pearls sewn into this headpiece, and Rebbe Zusia proceeded to remove them and gave them to the man.

Shortly thereafter, Rebbe Zusia's wife discovered what he had done, and shouted at him, "You gave away those pearls? Those are not imitation pearls! Those are genuine!"

Rebbe Zusia immediately ran after the man. "Listen!" he said. "Those pearls I gave you. They are genuine! Don't sell them cheaply!"

❧

I cannot sufficiently emphasize the impact upon me of the stories Father told.

I have no expertise in child development nor in educational psychology, but I have reason to believe that the most profound formation of character occurs in the very early years of one's life. I learned primarily by example and by stories, stories of the great *zaddikim* who Father so obviously venerated, and whose values were therefore to serve as the ideals toward which one must strive.

I cannot say what kind of impression some of these stories made upon me at the time I heard them. Retrospective vision is often very inaccurate. I do recall, however, reacting to the following story, which I must have heard before I was seven. I remember only that at the time I heard it, it bothered me, and that is enough to indicate that it had caused me to think. It made me think about things which probably do not affect most children under seven.

Father told about our ancestor, the great Maggid of Czernobl, who had always been extremely charitable and very lavish in his generosity. All at once, the Maggid underwent a total change of character. He became very strict with every kopek that went out of his hands. Those who had previously been the benefactors of his bounty were now turned away with little or nothing. This went so far that one day while praying, he happened to see a peasant woman gathering bits of kindling wood from his yard, and he rapped on the window, motioning to her to leave. After a period of time, the pattern changed again to boundless generosity and charity.

The Maggid explained, "I realized that my acts of *tzdaka* were the result of my emotional constitution. I was by nature sensitive, and it hurt me to see people in need, hungry, tattered and homeless. I was giving *tzdaka* to placate myself, to relieve my own discomfort and not because it was a Divine commandment.

"As noble as the acts of *tzdaka* may have been, they were but an emotional response. I was being directed by inherent impulses. The latter can be very dangerous. Today I may respond to one internal drive, and tomorrow to another. I was not in full control of my behavior. Who knows where following one's passions can lead? One must be a master over one's behavior.

"I therefore had only one option. I had to condition myself to become emotionally calloused and indifferent. I had to become unmoved by the plight of others. Now that I have achieved this, I can give *tzdaka* as I am supposed to do. I am no longer a pawn, at the mercy of my emotions."

I remember being irritated when I heard this story. What was wrong with doing something good, regardless of what the motivation was? But whether I liked it or disliked it, the message got across. Self-mastery must be achieved at all costs. The distinguishing feature between man and lower forms of life is not intellect, but spirituality and self-mastery. Animals are driven by impulses, and are stopped from fulfilling their desires only by brute force or fear of punishment. Man must be different. Animals are not free, since they cannot choose, but are driven by their passions. Man is not to be a slave, even unto himself. Man must be the master of himself in every way.

I do not know when I finally *learned* this, but I heard it before seven. Teaching by telling stories can be powerful.

⁂

The Rebbe of Talna cited the Talmud, which supports the colloquialism, "Poverty stalks the poor" (or "the rich grow richer, and the poor grow poorer") with the following *halacha.* When the offerings of the first-ripened fruits were brought to the Temple in old Jerusalem. the poor would bring them in baskets woven out of reeds, and the wealthy would bring them on trays of silver and gold. The silver and gold trays would be returned to the owners, but the woven reed baskets would be retained. Ergo, the rich retained their wealth, while the meager possessions of the poor were not returned to them.

"Where is the justice in this?" asked the Rebbe of Talna. Then he went on to explain, "But I fully understand this.

"One time," said the Rebbe, "I sent word to some of my *chassidim* that I would shortly be visiting their community. The *shtibel* (small synagogue, often comprised of the followers of a Rebbe) erupted in joy.

"Yankel returned home from the *shtibel* in euphoria, and told his wife that the Rebbe would soon be coming. Suddenly, Yankel's elation gave way to an expression of worry and sadness.

" 'What is it with you, Yankel?' the wife asked. 'Just a moment ago you were so overjoyed.'

"Yankel shook his head. 'Don't you know,' he said, 'the Rebbe collects for several of his favorite charities, like for the *hachnosas kalah* (enabling poor families to marry off their children), and I have nothing to donate!'

" 'Don't let that worry you,' the wife said. 'We still have several weeks, and God will help that you will earn a little extra. Also, I can do some baking and sell it off in the marketplace. I can also finish off some needlework, and we can put together something you can give the Rebbe.'

"Yankel's euphoria returned, and in the next few weeks, they gathered kopek by kopek. When I came to town, Yankel contributed his meager donation with gratitude and love.

"On the other hand," continued the Rebbe, "Boruch, the wealthiest man in the community, came home from services very glum.

"'What is it with you today?' his wife asked.

"'Oh,' Boruch said, 'They announced today that the Rebbe will be visiting soon. And don't you know, he'll put the touch on me for a hefty donation to charity. Another fifty rubles down the drain.'"

The Rebbe explained, "For the recipients of charity I had to accept Boruch's fifty rubles which were contributed grudgingly, but my true enjoyment was in receiving the few kopeks that Yankel and his wife had scraped together with love.

"I surmise," the Rebbe said, "that this is precisely what must have transpired in the days of the Temple.

"A pious peasant burst into his hut dancing with joy. He explained to his wife that the grapes in their tiny vineyard had begun to ripen, and so had the pomegranates and the dates on their few trees. 'It will soon be time to carry the fruits to the Sanctuary in Jerusalem on the Festival,' he beamed.

"Abruptly, his face fell and he turned morose. 'What has happened?' asked his wife, 'Is there anything wrong?'

"'It just occurred to me,' the husband said, 'we don't have a suitable container to carry the fruits to Jerusalem.'

"'Don't let that worry you,' the wife said. 'I will sit down with our daughter and weave you a beautiful reed basket that you will be proud of.' And indeed that night, mother and daughter began weaving a basket, with hearts full of gratitude that God enabled them to have a share in this *mitzvah.* The work was accompanied by songs of praise from the Psalms, so full of devotion that God silenced the hymns of the angels to listen to these sincere songs of worship. In due time the beautiful basket was completed, and when laden with the first ripened fruits, was accepted into the Sanctuary. The basket woven in love and devotion was an integral part of the offering and deserved to have a permanent place in the Divine presence.

"On the other hand," the Rebbe continued, "a wealthy man who owned many fields and orchards was alerted by one of his hired men. 'Some of the fruits of the orchards and vineyards are beginning to ripen,' he said.

'Well, what of it?' asked the wealthy man.

'That means it's time to carry the offering of the first-ripened fruits to the Sanctuary,' the hired man answered.

'Good God, not again!' his master exclaimed. 'I can't keep running back and forth to Jerusalem all the time. I've got too many things to take care of right here. Oh, well, if it has to be done, it just has to be done. Go ahead and designate the fruits I have to take up!' Then after a pause, he said, 'And one thing more. Last year that pompous Nachman from the Galilee tried to show off by bringing his offering on a fancy silver tray. Let's show him who's who! I'll bring my offering on a solid gold tray. That will make him turn green with envy.'

"You see," the Rebbe explained, "trays of gold and silver that were brought to spite others and to arouse their envy had no place in the Sanctuary, and were returned to their owners. The baskets woven of reeds, with every turn of the dexterous fingers motivated by the joy of fulfilling the Divine commandments, were prized and taken into the Sanctuary to remain in God's immediate presence."

IX

Parents and Children

There is something comforting about being a child. This feeling has nothing to do with being cared for in actuality, but simply with the identity of being a child.

How long is one a child? As long as one has a parent.

It would be well if parents understood this. Parents never outgrow their usefulness.

Not infrequently I see patients whose depressions are due to feelings of futility. Their children are grown, married, independent, and live far away from them. Particularly if the parents have retired from work and are no longer economically productive, they tend to feel that their existence is purposeless.

Nothing could be further from the truth. Parents should realize that their roles and functions may change, but not their purposefulness.

Parental roles are indeed constantly changing. When the children are infants, the function of the parent is to provide the essentials for survival: food, shelter, relief of discomfort, etc. As the children grow, they no longer need to be fed and diapered, but the parents provide for their sustenance, wash their clothes, keep house for them, teach them, and drive them from place to place.

As the children grow older and more independent, the parents may be their advisers and confidants. When the children reach the stage when all the supportive functions have ceased, the parents still serve a most important role. They are the ones with whom the children can share their achievements or those of their children.

When a new child is born, you call your parents and tell them. And you call them when the child sits, stands, walks, produces the first tooth. You call them when the child starts kindergarten, graduates grade school, high school, college, gets a promotion at work, or gets engaged. You call when there is anything you wish to share. No distress equals that of achieving something and not having anyone with whom to share your pride.

There is an apochryphal story about a not-so-pious rabbi who became a golf fanatic. He could not let one day go by without playing golf. When Yom Kippur came around, he was beside himself, because although playing golf on Yom Kippur should have been out of the question, he simply felt he could not survive twenty-four hours without playing golf. He therefore arose before dawn on Yom Kippur, and walked to the golf course, secure in the belief that he could play nine holes without being seen by anyone.

Up in Heaven, this created a furor. The angels could not contain their wrath at the desecration of Yom Kippur, and came before the Creator demanding instant retribution. "Shoot down a lightning bolt and kill the sinner," they said.

The Almighty responded, "Leave things to Me."

The angels stood by and watched as the rabbi took a swing . . . and made a hole-in-one.

In unison the angels emitted a loud scream, "What! This man desecrates the holiest day of the year and You reward him with a hole-in-one?"

To which the Creator responded, "Think, my hosts, think. To whom can he boast about it today?"

Yes, the distress of not having anyone with whom to share a personal achievement may be the worst suffering of all.

An elderly parent may be thousands of miles away, but as long as there is a parent, one can feel himself to be a child.

Shortly after arriving in America in 1927, Father visited Montreal, where there were a number of his *landsleit* (fellow Ukrainians). One man who visited him was eighty-six years old, and after a little conversation said, "Rabbi, would you pay a visit to my father?"

"Your father?" Father asked with astonishment.

"Yes," the man said. "My father is in the old folks' home. He is one hundred fourteen, although he denies it. He claims he is only one hundred twelve."

Father was thrilled at the prospect of meeting a man of that vintage. Accompanied by his attendant, he went to the home for the aged. The old man was resting in bed, obviously very feeble in body but alert in mind.

The old man told Father that he had personally known our ancestor, the Maggid of Czernobl, who died in 1832.

Father's attendant then said to the old man, "I would sure like to have your longevity."

The old man smiled and shook his head. "No, young man," he said. "You can't have *my* longevity because I need it for myself. You'd better have your own longevity."

The old man then turned to Father and asked, "Rabbi, did my *boychick'l* come to see you?"

Father used to enjoy telling of this encounter. A man of

eighty-six, a great-grandfather, was still a *"boychick'l"* because a parent existed whose child he was, regardless of his age.

❧

Father was disturbed by the increasing incidence of children placing their elderly parents in institutions for the aged. He felt that such facilities should be reserved for those individuals who were unfortunate in not having any children to look after them in their later years, but in cases where children had the means to maintain parents outside an institution, he was vehemently opposed to institutional placement. He recognized that the structure of the super-industrialized society and the increasing prevalence of both spouses being employed and away from the home all day would result in more elderly parents being put out to pasture, but could not make peace with this.

When people would seek Father's counsel about placing a parent in a facility for the elderly, he would respond with the following story.

A *zaddik* was once accompanied by a disciple on a stroll through the city, when they heard a cry of desperation coming from a nearby house. On investigation they found that a man was dragging his elderly father toward the door, intent on throwing him out of his house. The old man was crying and pleading for mercy, begging the son not to evict him.

The disciple was overcome with rage, and was shocked that his teacher, the *zaddik*, was doing nothing to stop this atrocious behavior. In fact, the *zaddik* stood calmly by the window observing the scene, as the old man's entreaties fell upon the unheeding ears of the son, who persisted in the eviction. The disciple felt compelled to put an end to this horrible behavior, but in deference to his master, he too remained silent.

Just as the son had pushed the elderly father over the threshold, the *zaddik* abruptly ran in, seized the son by the nape of the neck, and gave him a sound thrashing and scolding, chastising him for this gross insolence and cruelty toward his father.

After leaving the house, the *zaddik* turned to his disciple. "You are without doubt wondering why I remained silent as long as I did," he said. "You see, this elderly father in his younger years had attempted to throw his own father out of the house, and had succeeded in dragging him up to the threshold. Thus, he too deserved being dragged *up to* the threshold; but when he was dragged *beyond* the threshold—ah! That was more than he had deserved, and at that point, I intervened."

Father would then say, "Remember, whichever way you act toward your parents will serve as an example as to how your children will behave toward you when you grow old. Now you may do as you wish."

❧

To what degree must one carry out parental obedience?

We used to hear about the Zeide of Sanz who once became entangled on a question of law with his eldest son, Rebbe Chezkiel, who was a first-rate halachic authority. The two disagreed sharply, and in the heat of the argument, the Zeide said to Rebbe Chezkiel, "Don't ever set foot over my doorstep again."

Rebbe Chezkiel left the house via a window.

❧

There seem to be some rather weighty problems that have developed thanks to the marvels of medical science, which have prolonged the average life span and have thus greatly increased the number of elderly people in the population.

There are almost daily references in the newspapers to the crises confronting Medicare and the Social Security system, which are threatened with bankruptcy. A proposed solution of increasing Social Security taxes is met with resistance from the working population whose take-home pay appears to be dwindling, but decreasing benefits to the elderly is met with strong opposition by the senior citizens.

In addition to the very real fiscal difficulties are the attitudinal problems. Everyone feels not only that the needs of the elderly should be provided for adequately, but also that this must be done without grudge or resentment. It is of course impolitic to take any other position. Even at the individual level, many people totally repress their resentment. Whereas the support of a retired oldster was previously shared by seventeen younger working people, the burden now falls on only three. I believe that there would be better opportunities to solve some of the problems presented by the senior citizen segment of the population if we didn't have to conceal or repress our feelings.

Father would often quote Leibel as exemplifying a healthy attitude. I remember Leibel's father, a saintly looking old man with a long snow-white beard. Leibel's father lived with him for many years after his mother's death, and Leibel accorded his father honor and service usually given only to kings.

My father held up Leibel as an example of what filial

devotion should be, but never failed to quote Leibel as having said to his father, "Pa, I would never give you away for a million dollars, but I wouldn't give a nickel for another one of you."

In one breath, the love, admiration, and devotion for the father coexisted with a conscious realization of the hardship which caring for him was causing. The two are not incompatible, and indeed, recognition of the latter may allow the former to be felt and manifested in greater intensity.

❧

My late adolescence and early adulthood was in that era when everyone over 35 was considered to be either senile or ignorant. The wisdom of youth was sovereign. Accepting the guidance or counseling of one's parents was considered to be the epitome of folly.

I, however, was reared in the ancient and traditional belief that the experiences of life are the wisest teachers, and that parents who may have less book learning are nevertheless, on the whole, wiser than their children.

Father used to tell us of an uncle whom he greatly admired, and Father's admiration was a definitive seal of approval of the uncle's value system.

Before getting to this tale, a word of background is necessary. Among many chassidic families in Europe, arranged marriages were the rule. Bride and groom met *after* the wedding rather than before. Engagements were often sealed when the parties were children. I recall that at my oldest son's Bar Mitzvah, when Father put the *tfillin* on him for the first time, he jokingly said, "You should be ashamed of yourself. When I put on *tfillin*, I was already engaged for two years."

Great-grandfather arranged marriages for his children via intermediaries who were people close to him whose judgment he respected, much like the Patriarch Abraham and his servant Eliezer. When it came to arrange a match for the youngest child, Great-grandmother objected. Boruch was the darling of the family, and no stranger would be entrusted with choosing a wife for him. For Boruch, Great-grandmother herself would travel about and choose a wife. This mission was carried out, and Great-grandmother returned home with the Mazel Tov tidings.

Some time later, Boruch's bride-to-be came to a nearby village, and his sisters went to meet her. They returned in virtual mourning, because the young lady was most unattractive. What had Mother done, to choose for beloved Boruch someone so unbecoming?

Great-grandfather was very upset, and immediately sent a message to the *michuten* (the bride's father) requesting that the young couple meet face to face.Among chassidic families this was unheard of, and such a suggestion by anyone of lesser stature and authority than the Rebbe would have been totally rejected.

Boruch did not approve of the encounter. Mother had chosen for him, and certainly had chosen wisely. There was no need for his approval. Great-grandfather, observing the concern of the other children, had to order Boruch, with the injunction of parental obedience, to meet with the young lady. If he did not approve, the engagement would be dissolved.

Boruch had to obey his father's command. He walked into the room, greeted the young lady, wished her a safe journey home, and left. To his parents and anxious sisters he said only, "If Mother said this was the right wife for me, then I approve of her choice."

Uncle Boruch and his wife had a long and happy marriage, much richer in love and devotion than many of those that were founded on more romantic grounds.

That one must honor one's parents I learned from the Ten Commandments. That one should trust his parents I learned from Father's esteem for Uncle Boruch.

X

Chassidic Tales

Chassidim love to relate stories about the great chassidic masters. Many of these are accounts of wondrous deeds performed by the *zaddik,* or blessings that were dramatically fulfilled.

Thinking back about the stories my father used to relate, I see that most of them were not merely accounts of miraculous deeds, but of the greatness of character and devotion achieved by the *zaddikim,* or of the virtues of Jews.

Father's *ahavas yisroel* (love for a fellow Jew) knew no bounds. He would tell of his grandfather, who once stated, "If any Jew feels a pain even in his little finger, I feel that pain." Father could not tolerate any condemnation of a Jew. In the many trials or disagreements over which he presided as judge or arbitrator, people would sometimes refer to someone who had wronged them as being a bad or wicked person. Father would have none of that.

"There is no such entity as a bad or wicked Jew," Father would say. "Every Jew has a *neshama* which is of Divine origin, and the essence of every Jew is good. When a Jew behaves improperly, it is because he does not understand that what he is doing is wrong, and in the final analysis, harmful to himself. If he misbehaves, it is out of ignorance of this, and he is to be pitied for his lack of understanding rather than condemned for wickedness."

I believe that it was because he wished to emphasize that one should never pass harsh judgment over a fellow Jew that Father told the story of the three trials that came before the great Rebbe Levi Yitzchok of Berdichev. I heard this story countless times, yet it never grew old nor boring.

In Berdichev there lived a wealthy man, one Isaac Boruchovich, who had a reputation in the community as being a miser. He never contributed to community projects, and it was impossible to extract any contributions from him for charitable causes. Consequently, when Boruchovich died, the community leaders saw their opportunity to coerce the family to compensate for all his derelictions. They simply told the family that Boruchovich would not be accorded burial until the heirs made a sizable contribution from his vast estate to the community coffers.

According to Jewish law, delay of burial is a most serious transgression. Once the soul departs from the body, it is prescribed that the latter be returned to the earth from whence it was derived with the greatest expedience possible. It is considered a desecration of the departed as well as a suffering for the soul to delay burial.

When word of the community's action reached Rebbe Levi Yitzchok, he ordered that Boruchovich be given proper burial without the slightest delay. Furthermore, he wished to be informed when the funeral would be held, and stated that he wished to accompany the funeral party until the completion of the burial.

The community was dumbfounded. Rebbe Levi Yitzchok's advocacy on behalf of Boruchovich was mysterious enough, but his participation in the funeral to the very end was completely incomprehensible. Even for respected and more deserving members of the community, Rebbe Levi Yitzchok would escort the bier for a short distance and then return promptly to his studies, so as not to be detached from his immersion in Torah. Yet, here for Boruchovich, of all people, the Rebbe was going to spend all that time until completion of the burial!

After returning from the cemetery, the Rebbe, sensing the community's bewilderment, called the leaders into his study. "Boruchovich," the Rebbe said, "appeared before me as a litigant in three trials, all of which he lost."

The First Trial

Berdichev was the commercial center for the many small villages and towns in the area. Since travel in those days was cumbersome, merchants in the smaller communities would designate a person to do all their purchasing for them. They would give him the money, and he would bring them their desired merchandise from Berdichev.

One time such a purchasing agent, while making a transaction in the marketplace, suddenly discovered that he had lost his money belt. The awareness that he had lost such a vast sum for which he was personally liable and for which he could never compensate was more than he could bear, and he fell away in a faint. As soon as he would come to and realize his calamity, he would emit a loud wail and again faint.

Boruchovich, who happened to be on his way to *shul*, noticed the crowd that had gathered, and his curiosity led him to inquire about what was going on. Upon being informed, he pushed his way through the crowd, and the next time the man came to, he shouted, "Don't worry, my friend. I have found your money belt! It is safe."

Upon hearing the glad tidings, the man's spirit returned. The pallor yielded as the blood circulation to his face returned, and he sat up.

"Now, look," Boruchvich said. "I have found a money belt, and in all likelihood, it is the one you lost. But obviously, you must give me adequate identification so that I know I am returning it to its true owner."

The man described the style and color of the money belt. "Yes," said Boruchovich. "But that is a standard type of money belt, and many merchants have similar ones. Can you give me more precise identification, such as how much money it contained, and in what denominations?"

Without delay, the man promptly reported the exact number of bills he had, in hundreds, fifties, etc. Boruchovich then said, "I am on my way to *shul* now, but you can ask any of the many townspeople here about my trustworthiness. I will return from *shul* in about an hour, and you can then come to my home. I have declared in front of all these people that I found a money belt such as you describe, and they can testify to this, so you needn't worry that I will later deny it. If the contents of the belt correspond to the amounts you enumerated, I will gladly return it to you."

Boruchovich continued on as if to go to *shul,* but then took off on a side street and made his way to a store where he purchased a money belt such as the man had described. He then went home and filled it with the number of bills in the various denominations the man had enumerated. When the man came to his home, Boruchovich informed him that the money in the belt indeed corresponded with his account, and gladly turned the belt over to him.

The man was so elated that he had been saved from utter disaster that in his euphoria, he failed to notice that the belt was brand new, where his belt was well worn.

Word of the incident spread through Berdichev, and the person who had in truth found and kept the lost money belt was plagued by remorse. How could he unjustly keep the money when its loss had driven another person to insensibility? How could he keep this money when a total stranger had given such a vast sum of his own to save this man's sanity? The torment gave him no peace, and finally he took the money belt, and after locating the owner, he confessed that he had initially been unable to withstand the temptation of enrichment, and then surrendered the money belt to him.

The purchasing agent immediately noted that this worn money belt was indeed his, and that Boruchovich's belt was a new one. He thanked the finder, and then made his way to Boruchovich to return the latter's money, since he now had his own. But Boruchovich refused to accept the money, and suggested he return the old belt to its finder. "God provided me with an opportunity for a *mitzvah*," he said, "and I will not have it taken away from me." The finder, however, was equally adamant that after his initial weakness in yielding to temptation, he did not wish to be unjustly enriched, and he refused to accept the money. They then agreed to abide by Rebbe Levi Yitzchok's decision.

After listening to the entire account, Rebbe Levi Yitzchok ruled against Boruchovich, i.e., that he must accept the return of his money. But, the Rebbe ruled, the *mitzvah* of returning a lost object belonged to Boruchovich, and not to the finder. Thus, Boruchovich lost this trial.

The Second Trial

One of the well-to-do merchants in Berdichev had suffered a severe turn of fortune, and had lost everything he owned. For months he was depressed and completely incapacitated. Finally, he gathered enough courage to try his luck again in business. However, he had no capital with which to start his venture.

The merchant contacted Boruchovich and asked him for a loan. "I know you to be an upright and honest person," Boruchovich said, "but surely, you don't expect me to lend you such a sizable sum without a guarantor."

"I have a guarantor," the merchant replied.

"Fine," Boruchovich said. "I will draw up the note, and as soon as your guarantor co-signs it, I will give you the money."

"I cannot get a signature from my guarantor," the merchant said. "You see, God is my guarantor. I am sure that He will not fail me."

Boruchovich was taken by surprise. After a moment's hesitation, he said, "Good. I accept your guarantor. Here is your loan, and it is to be repaid at the end of a year."

During the next year, the merchant's business ventures were blessed with success. He happened to be away from Berdichev on the day the payment of the loan was due, but several days later, came to Boruchovich with the payment in full.

Boruchovich shook his head. "No," he said. "I cannot accept your money. You see, your guarantor has already paid me, and I cannot accept double payment."

"I don't understand," the merchant said.

Boruchovich explained. "I was negotiating a deal to buy a large quantity of lumber. It was a very profitable transaction for me, but I lost out to a competitive bidder. I had already put the whole subject out of my mind. On the day your note was due, I received word that my competitor had suddenly and inexplicably withdrawn from the transaction, and that the deal was mine. Needless to say, I was overjoyed.

"When I calculated my profit on the deal, it was exactly equal to the amount of your loan. Obviously, this could not be a coincidence. I could only conclude that your guarantor had decided to pay off your debt. Duplicate payment I will not accept," Boruchovich said.

The merchant protested. "Look," he said. "I have been very fortunate in business this year. I will be eternally grateful for your kindness in granting me the loan, but now that I am doing well, I do not wish to be a recipient of charity which I certainly do not need. You must accept my payment."

Unable to reach an agreement, they concurred to abide by the decision of Rebbe Levi Yitzchok.

The Rebbe ruled against Boruchovich, namely, that he must accept the merchant's payment. "Nevertheless," the Rebbe said, "Boruchovich retains the entire *mitzvah* as though he had given the money to charity."

Boruchovich lost the second trial.

The Third Trial

In Berdichev there lived a man who struggled to eke out a meager living for his family. He had grandiose aspirations, and repeatedly told his wife that if he could go to Leipzig for a year, he was certain he could do well in that commercial metropolis, and bring back enough capital to establish himself in business locally, and that they would then be able to live in comfort.

The wife would not hear of this. "Is it not enough that we are impoverished? And what if when you go to a distant land, and God forbid, something happens to you, then I and the children are forever stranded to be a widow and orphans?* And what would we live from if you leave? Am I to go from door to door begging alms?"

One day the man came home with good news. "I have been hired by Boruchovich to represent his interests in Leipzig," he said. "He will pay me well. Every Friday you are to report to his office to receive my salary until I return. But I must leave immediately, since he is negotiating several major deals there now."

The wife, assured of more than adequate sustenance for her family, helped her husband pack his things, and within a short time, he was on his way to Leipzig.

On Friday, the woman reported to Boruchovich's office as instructed, and gave the cashier her husband's name. The cashier was perplexed. "We don't have anyone by that name in our employ," he said.

The woman told the cashier that her husband had been hired by Boruchovich just that week to represent his interests in Leipzig. The cashier checked his records again, and then told the woman that she was mistaken, because they

*According to Jewish law, if a husband disappears, even for many years, he cannot be declared legally dead. Thus, unless there is reliable evidence of his death, the wife can never remarry. In the days when travel to a distant country was hazardous, this was a formidable risk.

had no record of anyone by that name being added to the payroll.

The woman suddenly realized that her husband had deceived her, and had contrived the story to gain her permission to leave. Her worst fears had come true. She was now alone and destitute. She began to weep loudly and bitterly.

Boruchovich, who was working in his office, heard the crying and came out to investigate what was going on. The cashier then explained to him that this woman had been duped by her husband, who, in order to persuade her to permit him to go to Leipzig, had fabricated a story that Boruchovich had hired him, and that she was to collect his pay weekly.

"Oh, for heaven's sake," said Boruchovich. "It had totally slipped my mind to inform you," he said to the cashier. Then he turned to the woman and said, "Your husband told you the truth. My agent in Leipzig recently died, and earlier this week, I met your husband, and after some discussion, I did hire him to go to Leipzig. But I had so many things on my mind that I forgot to tell the cashier to place him on the payroll. Yes, you are to come every Friday for his pay."

More than a year passed, during which the husband in Leipzig had been successful in business, and returned to Berdichev with adequate funds to establish himself in business. He knew that he would find his family destitute, his wife and children hungry and in rags, living off charity. He knew he would be greeted by a shower of maledictions from the wife whom he had deceived and deserted. However, he hoped he would ultimately be forgiven for his deception by now being able to provide amply for them, which he could never have achieved had he not gone to Leipzig.

Imagine his astonishment when his wife and children,

well-dressed and well-fed, gave him a warm welcome. After a bit, he cautiously inquired how they had been able to manage so well in his absence. His wife seemed surprised by his questions. She told him that she had followed his instructions and received weekly pay from Boruchovich.

The following day, the husband calculated how much she had received, and went to Boruchovich to repay him. He explained that while he regretted having lied to his wife, this had been the only means by which he could go to Leipzig where he knew he could prosper, as he indeed had. He was deeply appreciative of Boruchovich's noble gesture in supporting his family. However, he now had ample funds and did not wish his family to be recipients of charity; hence, he was returning the amount of money that Boruchovich had provided, with unending gratitude.

Boruchovich refused to accept the money. "I had a *mitzvah* of sustaining an entire family both physically and emotionally. I will not sell this *mitzvah* for money." They were both adamant in their respective positions, and agreed to abide by Rebbe Levi Yitzchok's decision.

Rebbe Levi Yitzchok ruled against Boruchovich, that he must accept repayment from the husband. "However," he said, "he retains the entire *mitzvah* as though it had been entirely at his expense."

Rebbe Levi Yitzchok then said to the community leaders, "You knew one Boruchovich; I knew another aspect of the man. Anyone who loses three trials such as these does not deserve the insult of having his burial delayed."

I am certain that the message of this tale was not only that we should not prejudge anyone, but also that we should not come to any conclusions about any Jew even with what appears to be adequate evidence. Not all diamonds reveal their glitter. Some are covered with mud and debris, but they are no less precious.

❧

The Baal Shem Tov and his immediate disciples encountered enormous opposition toward their teachings and practices. For various reasons, many noted scholars of that era suspected the Baal Shem Tov of deviating from traditional Judaism, and waged a fierce battle against chassidim. Unfortunately, the disagreements between chassidim and their opponents (misnagdim) later assumed the character of tribal feuds, far from the pure motives of the original parties.

Father used to tell a story of the Baal Shem Tov which shed light on those original adversaries.

The city of Brody in Poland was a citadel of the misnagdim, and the great Talmudist, Rebbe Chaim Zanser of Brody, was among them. One time when the Baal Shem Tov visited Brody, the zealous misnagdim took after him with a vengeance. Rebbe Chaim Zanser, although sympathizing with them, was not wont to do physical battle, and remained behind in the house of study.

Later that day a woman called upon Rebbe Chaim to pass judgment over a question which would determine her permissibility to have relations with her husband, and after studying the question, Rebbe Chaim ruled in the affirmative.

That night before retiring, Rebbe Chaim reviewed the events of that day, as was his custom every night, to see whether all his actions of that day were as they should have been, or perhaps there were things upon which he should improve. As he pondered the question of law regarding family purity which the woman had raised, it suddenly occurred to him that he had ruled incorrectly. He recognized that his ruling had undoubtedly resulted in the occurrence of a forbidden relationship. He had thus been responsible for causing another person to inadvertently transgress.

Rebbe Chaim was beside himself with self-flagellation. How could he have overlooked the correct ruling? He decided that this oversight could only have resulted from some misdeed, some transgression which he himself had committed, which had brought this mistaken judgment in its aftermath.

But what? Rebbe Chaim began to scrutinize his past behavior, to find what he had done wrong, what sin he had committed that had resulted in so serious a consequence as a distortion of judgment that had led an innocent person astray. But search as he might, he could find no misdeeds except for one: he had failed to join his colleagues in pursuing the Baal Shem Tov.

As dawn broke, Rebbe Chaim arose, and went out to the street to fill his pockets with stones with which he would pelt the Baal Shem Tov. After searching among the many inns in the city, he found where the Baal Shem Tov had spent the night, and hurried to atone for his dereliction. But when he met the Baal Shem Tov, the latter was reciting the prayers upon arising, and the saintly image of the Baal Shem Tov precluded any stone throwing.

After completing the prayers, the Baal Shem Tov greeted Rebbe Chaim. "*Shalom Aleichem,* Rebbe of Brody," the Baal Shem Tov said. "You have no reason to worry. Your ruling was perfectly sound!" And the Baal Shem Tov proceeded to review the question of law involved to Rebbe Chaim's satisfaction that his original ruling had indeed been correct, and that it was rather his reconsideration that had been erroneous.

Rebbe Chaim, overjoyed that he had not after all been the cause of anyone's transgression, left the inn and emptied his pockets of the stones that he had gathered. But as he did so, the Baal Shem Tov followed him, picking up the stones, kissing them, and putting them in his bosom. "Stones that were gathered with *kedusha* (holy motivation) dare not roll in the dust. These stones, too, have become sacred, and they should be stored with other objects of *mitzvah*."

This was my earliest impression of chassidim and misnagdim, men of divergent views, perhaps bitter adversaries, but whose dedication to sincerity and truth superseded any personal considerations.

❧

A woman came to the Maggid of Czernobl. "Please help me, holy Rebbe," she pleaded. "I have been married for ten years but have not yet had a child. Please bless me."

The Maggid sighed, "I am sorry, my dear child," he said, "but I cannot help you. There is nothing I can do for you."

"But everyone says that if you go to the great *zaddik* of Czernobl, you will be helped," the woman said. "You have helped so many others, why do you turn me down?"

The Maggid only shook his head. "I'm sorry. I can do nothing for you."

After the woman left, the Rebbe's *gabbai* (attendant) could not contain himself. "I cannot understand!" he said. "Why did you deny her a *bracha* (blessing)? What harm could it have done if you had blessed her?"

"You will soon see," said the Maggid. "Just wait a few moments, then go after her and call her back."

A few moments later, the tearful woman was brought to the Maggid. "Tell me, my child," the Maggid said. "What did you do after you left me?"

"What could I do?" the woman responded. "I lifted my eyes to heaven and I said, 'Dear God, I have no one else to rely on except You. Even the Rebbe has turned me down. You are the only one who can help me.' "

The Maggid smiled. "Go home in peace," he replied. "You shall have your child. You see, you misunderstood the nature of a blessing. You thought that the Rebbe has some magical powers to grant wishes. Only God can answer prayers. A Rebbe can assist the person with prayer, but you must understand that help can come only from the Almighty Himself.

"It was evident to me that you were misplacing your trust. You thought that I could perform some miracle for you. When I turned you away, you then prayed to God for help. You placed your hope and trust where it belongs, and your prayer will now be answered."

Another time, the interaction between the Maggid and a supplicant took a different course.

A man came to the Maggid and unburdened himself of his many worries and troubles. The Maggid listened sympathetically, then said "Have faith in God, and He will certainly help you."

The man was not satisfied. "That is not what the holy *sidur* says," the man complained. "I *daven* everyday, and in my *sidur* is says that God helped the Israelites from the hands of the Egyptians, and the Israelites *then* had faith in God. First He must help, and *then* we believe."

The Maggid smiled. "You are right," he said. "Even the Almighty is obligated to follow what the holy *sidur* says. Your prayers will be answered."

The Maggid explained, "This man's piety was simple and sincere. He was not manipulating. He was not conniving. His relationship with God was open and without reservation. This trust warrants the Divine blessing."

◆§ §◆

We hear much these days about "cover-ups" and attempts to suppress evidence. As one might guess, these are not new phenomena.

Father used to tell of one of the *zaddikim*, whose name escapes me, who stopped off at an inn accompanied by some of his chassidim. In the morning they were served breakfast, and after the Rebbe tasted the cereal,he remarked how good it was and asked for a second portion. When this was finished, he requested more, and this went on until he was told that all the cereal was gone.

The chassidim observed this with wonderment. The Rebbe usually ate very little, hardly enough to sustain himself. What had happened that he had suddenly developed a voracious appetite?

One of the chassidim eventually was bold enough to ask the Rebbe about the reason for his unusual behavior.

"Quite simple," the Rebbe said. "When I tasted the cereal, it tasted of kerosene. It was obvious that the cook, a poor orphaned girl working for her keep at the inn, had mistakenly put kerosene into the cereal instead of oil. Had this been discovered, the innkeeper would surely have dismissed this young woman. I had no choice other than to prevent this from happening by eating all the cereal."

There are cover-ups and there are cover-ups.

⁂

The Talmud teaches, "Judge every person in a favorable light" (Ethics of the Fathers I: 6), i.e., give everyone the benefit of the doubt.

Looking at everyone favorably was most characteristic of Father. This was why we heard so much of the great chassidic master, Rebbe Levi Yitzchok of Berdichev.

The Berdichever was not satisfied with simply assuming everyone to be innocent until proven guilty. He took it upon himself to seek out the meritorious qualities in everyone, and to serve as man's advocate before God, to prove to God that His children were deserving of Divine beneficence.

During the Berdichever's time, the political relationship between Russia and Turkey was a hostile one, and all Turkish merchandise was considered contraband in Russia. The penalty for possession of Turkish goods ranged from long imprisonment to death.

One Passover night before the Seder, the Berdichever told his congregation that he cannot begin the Seder without some Turkish snuff, and ordered them to find some Turkish snuff for him.

"But, Rebbe," the followers responded, "you know that Turkish tobacco is forbidden. No one would risk the punishment of possessing Turkish snuff."

"No matter," the Rebbe answered, "I must have Turkish snuff."

The people dispersed, and before long brought the Rebbe some Turkish snuff which someone had concealed.

"Good," said the Rebbe, "now I must have some fine Turkish wool. I want a bolt of woolen cloth from Turkey."

"An impossible request," the people said. "No one is foolish enough to own Turkish material today."

"Then there shall be no Seder," the Berdichever said. "We do not begin the Seder unless you bring the Turkish wool."

Again the crowd dispersed, and eventually brought the contraband wool to the Rebbe.

"Good," the Rebbe said. "Now bring me a piece of bread from a Jewish home."

"But, Rebbe," the followers answered. "Tonight is Passover. There is no bread in any Jewish home."

"Never mind," said the Rebbe. "You searched until you found other contraband. Go search for the bread."

After an extensive search, the people returned empty-handed. Nowhere in Berdichev was there to be found a Jewish household that had a morsel of bread.

The Berdichever was ecstatic. He lifted his eyes toward Heaven. "Look, *Ribono Shel Olam* (Master of the Universe)! The Czar has a mighty army and well-armed police that are permitted to shoot on sight anyone who defies his laws. He has ordered that under penalty of death, no one dare possess any Turkish goods. Yet when I wanted Turkish snuff, it was to be had. I wanted Turkish wool, and it, too, was to be found. But You, dear God, You do not have an army. No one fears that he will be shot on sight or imprisoned. Yet You have said that no one is to have *chometz* in their possession tonight, and not a single crumb can be found in a Jewish home. Their love and devotion for You far exceeds the fear of mortal punishment. Tell me, *Ribono Shel Olam,* with such devotion from Your children, do they not deserve better treatment than You have been according them?"

One time on the fast day of *Tisha-B'av,* the Rebbe of Berdichev came across an obviously non-observant Jew who was eating.

"My child," the Rebbe said, "You must certainly have forgotten that today is *Tisha-B'av,* a fast day."

"No, I did not forget," the man replied. "I know it is *Tisha-B'av,*" he said, continuing to eat.

"Ah, then, you certainly have not been feeling well, and you are under doctor's orders not to fast today," the Rebbe said.

"I am perfectly healthy," the man said, "And I have nothing to do with doctors."

The Berdichever lifted his face toward Heaven. "Look, *Ribono Shel Olam,* how truthful and honest Your children are. I have offered the man opportunities to explain away his behavior, but he insists on telling the truth even to his own hurt. He knows how much You value truth, and he will not divert from it. Who else would be so loyal to your principles?"

Rightly did the Great Rebbe Baruch of Medziboz say, "According to Rebbe Levi Yitzchok, God has not fulfilled His obligation toward even one Jew." Rebbe Levi Yitzchok considered every Jew to be precious and deserving of much greater reward than he receives.

❧

"The sincere devotion of the heart, that is what the Almighty desires." So taught the Baal Shem Tov.

Those who opposed the founder of chassidus distorted

this teaching to mean that the Baal Shem Tov did not insist on total compliance with the behavioral dictum of the *Shulchan Aruch* (code of Jewish law). Nothing could be further from the truth. What the Baal Shem Tov did mean is illustrated in the following story.

A pious Jew once came to Rebbe Michel of Zlotchowa and confessed that he had inadvertently violated the *Shabbos*. Realizing how serious an offense this was, he asked Rebbe Michel what was required for atonement.

Rebbe Michel expounded on the sanctity of the *Shabbos*, and how violation of the *Shabbos* is equivalent to rejection of the entire Torah. He told the man that he must fast on each Monday and Thursday for a full year, as an act of contrition.

Some time later, the man came to the Baal Shem Tov who told him that it was not necessary to fast. Rather, he said, the man should take it upon himself to be more cautious than ever in his observance of the *Shabbos*, should spend the entire *Shabbos* in prayer, in reciting the Psalms, or in joining in the study of the Torah, and should avoid thinking about his work or business affairs on the *Shabbos*.

The Baal Shem Tov then sent a message to Rebbe Michel, inviting him to come and spend *Shabbos* with him.

Rebbe Michel set out with more than enough time to spare, but his trip was dogged by every possible complication. First, the horse took a wrong turn in the road, then they were stopped by a severe rain and hail storm, then they were stuck in the mud, then an axle of the wagon broke. He did not reach the Baal Shem Tov's home until quite late Friday afternoon. Fearful that it was drawing close to sundown, he ran with great haste into the house, only to find the Baal Shem Tov standing with his *kiddush* cup in his hand, reciting the *kiddush* of *Shabbos.*

Assuming that *Shabbos* had already begun, and that he had thus violated the *Shabbos* by travelling, Rebbe Michel fell away in a faint. When he came to, the Baal Shem Tov was at his side. Rebbe Michel began to weep. "I have violated the sacred *Shabbos,*" he cried.

"No," the Baal Shem Tov said. "It is not yet evening. I had decided to inaugurate the *Shabbos* much earlier today. For you it was not yet *Shabbos.* You have done no wrong."

After Rebbe Michel regained his composure, the Baal Shem Tov said, "Tell me, do you now realize what kind of pangs of pain and remorse a Jew feels when he believes that he has violated the *Shabbos?*

"What is it that the Almighty desires," asked the Baal Shem Tov, "other than that one sincerely regret and repent any wrong one has done? If this sincere remorse is felt, there is no need for fasting or other self-flagellation. You must realize that a person who comes to you to ask for contrition has indeed sincerely regretted his transgression, and his atonement has essentially been accomplished."

This is what the Baal Shem Tov taught about sincerity and devotion being that which God desires.

❧

We were really not subjected to any fatalistic philosophy. Quite the contrary, we were always taught that with sincere prayer, one may reverse any decree. Yet, there seemed to be no getting away from the belief that certain things were "*bashert;*" i.e., if they were destined to be, they would be.

Father used to tell about the two great chassidic masters, the brothers Rebbe Elimelech and Rebbe Zusia, who subjected themselves to several years of self-imposed exile and wandering to atone for what they considered their "sins."

After an exhausting day of walking (since they had no means to afford travelling by wagon), they retired at an inn, and lay down to rest on the benches near the pot-bellied stove. Soon the peasant-folk came in after the day's work, and began relaxing by drinking, imbibing sufficiently to become convivial and giddy, soon beginning to dance around in a circle. As they passed the two men lying on the benches, one of the drunken men would take a swat at Rebbe Zusia, and this was repeated with each revolution.

Then Rebbe Elimelech said to his brother, "Zusia, why should you always be the one to be beaten? I have some coming to me, too. Let us trade places."

The next time the circle swung around and the drunken man was about to land his blow, his friend stopped him. "Stepan," he said, "it is not right that you always hit the one on this bench. This time, give it to the one on the other bench."

Rebbe Zusia was again the recipient of the blows and said, "Elimelech, if it is *bashert* for Zusia to get whipped, then Zusia will get whipped. There is no outsmarting Him."

❧

Father was very fond of the noted scholar, Rebbe Meir Shapiro of Lubin. When Father was but a newlywed, residing in Cracow, Rebbe Meir came to Father's modest apartment on Friday night to sit at his *Shabbos* table. This gesture was essentially one of acknowledging Father as a Rebbe, to whose *Shabbos* table followers would come. It was a most encouraging support to an unknown young man, still wet behind the ears, to be given public recognition by a noted rabbinic leader of the stature of Rebbe Meir.

Father held Rebbe Meir in very high esteem. He told us of an incident when Rebbe Meir was returning from a conference in which the foremost rabbinic leaders and scholars had participated. All of the participants were travelling on the same train, and at each station the local Jewish populace came to pay homage to their leaders. All the great *zaddikim* of the time went out to greet the crowd, all except the *Chafetz Chayim* (Rabbi Israel Meir Hacohen) who remained behind in the coach.

Rebbe Meir, who was still a very young man compared to the aged *Chafetz Chayim,* approached the sage. "Why are you not going out to greet the people?" he asked. "They are clamoring to see you."

"Why should they wish to look at me?" asked the *Chafetz Chayim,* who was the paragon of humility. "Do I look any different from any other person? They only wish to see me because they have the erroneous opinion that I am some kind of *zaddik.* And if I were to go out to them, I would be confirming that delusion. 'Here, look at me! I am someone special! I am unique!' And that is conceit and vanity."

"Let me concede for the moment that this would be conceit and vanity," Rebbe Meir said. "What is so wrong with conceit and vanity?"

The *Chafetz Chayim* appeared astonished by the questions. "Why, conceit and vanity are sinful," he said, "disgusting sins."

"And what is so terrible about a sin?" asked Rebbe Meir.

"What are you saying?" challenged the *Chafetz Chayim.* "For our sins, we will be condemned to the tortures of Hell."

"And so you will suffer a bit in Hell," Rebbe Meir responded. "But your people out there wish to see you, and they will enjoy seeing you. You wish to deny them their wish and pleasure just to save yourself a bit of discomfort in Hell!"

The *Chafetz Chayim* was electrified by Rebbe Meir's comment. As the train slowed down before the next station, he was the first one out on the platform to greet the waiting crowd, and so for every station thereafter. His personal suffering was a small sacrifice if it would provide enjoyment for others.

❧

Our great-uncle, the Rebbe of Talna, was renowned for his wit and wisdom, and Father used to enjoy relating stories which demonstrated the validity of his reputation. This story was one of his favorites.

One of the Talna Rebbe's followers had begun to exhibit some very unusual behavior, and the wife, who was very worried that her husband was going insane, insisted that he visit the Rebbe for consultation and guidance. The husband resisted at first, but finally acquiesced with one stipulation: he must be allowed to talk with the Rebbe privately first. The wife readily agreed.

Upon meeting with the Rebbe in private, the husband said, "Rebbe, I am in deep trouble. My wife has gone out of her mind. Although she behaves normally in every other way, she has developed this delusion and is obsessed with the idea that I have gone crazy. She gives me no peace and torments me, insisting that I am insane. In just a minute, she will come in, and I am sure she will complain that I have gone mad. Now, Rebbe, you can talk with me as long as you wish, and see for yourself whether there is anything wrong with my mind."

A few moments later the wife was ushered in and promptly began telling the Rebbe how her husband had gone out of his mind, and how she was suffering from his madness. As she was doing so, the husband gestured to the Rebbe, as if to say, "See, just as I told you. She is out of her mind with this delusion about me."

The Rebbe listened attentively, then said, "Look, this is a most difficult case. Each of you is claiming that the other has taken leave of his/her sense, yet both of you are coherent. This will take some analysis. But before we get to that," the Rebbe said, "I'm going to ask as my fee that you make a donation to a charitable fund for which I am collecting."

The husband turned to the wife. "Go ahead, Esther," he said. "You heard what the Rebbe said. Give the Rebbe some money for charity."

As the wife reached for her purse, the Rebbe said, "Well, that settles the case." And turning to the husband, he said, "If she is the one that handles all the money, then you must be the one that is out of his mind."

❧

Father used to love to tell the story of the *zaddik* of Ropsicz and his Rebetzin.

It seems that the Rebetzin was a very frugal woman. She kept everything in the house under lock and key. All the cupboards were tightly secured lest anyone help themselves to her provisions.

The Rebetzin was a most devout and pious woman. She prayed regularly, and when involved in prayer, meditated so profoundly that she entered into a trance-like state. Even an earthquake would not have distracted her.

When she prepared the *kugel* for *Shabbos* she was most austere with the ingredients, and added just the bare minimum of *schmaltz.* Her husband, the *zaddik* Rebbe Naftali, would wait until she began to pray, and knowing that while in deep meditation she would be oblivious to everything, he would remove the cupboard keys from her apron pocket, gain access to the *schmaltz,* add a generous amount to the *kugel,* and then return the keys to their place. The Rebetzin remained thoroughly unaware of this.

On *Shabbos,* when the *kugel* was served, dripping with abundant *schmaltz,* she would say to her husband,"See, you always criticize me for being too austere in my cooking. Just look at that *kugel.* It is overflowing with *schmaltz.*"

Rebbe Naftali would nod and say, "Yes, my dear wife. This is a reward, a blessing from Heaven. God has rewarded us with a bountiful *kugel.* This reward comes to us by virtue of your sincere prayers and my good deeds."

❧ ❧

Among my character defects is an intolerance for stupidity. I do not take full responsibility for this, since I inherited this trait from an ancestor, the Rebbe of Ropsicz.

Rebbe Naftali of Ropsicz, a man of infinite tolerance, had no room whatever for stupidity. He used to say that even if he will see a fool escorted to the loftiest berths in Paradise, he will shout after him, "A fool is a fool, and remains a fool forever."

People would ask him why he was so harsh with fools. After all, a person is not to blame for being stupid. Does not the Talmud state that before a person's birth it is decreed whether he will be short or tall, rich or poor, wise or stupid? It is thus not the fool's fault that he is that which he is, for it was so decreed.

To this Rebbe Naftali replied, "But it is also decreed that on Passover one must eat *matzah*. Yet, it is not required that one eat an enormous quantity to comply with the order of the Torah. All that is necessary to fulfill the *mitzvah* is that one eat a small piece of *matzah*, no greater than the size of an olive.

"Well then, granted that there was a Divine decree that this person be stupid. Could he not have satisfied the Divine decree with a bare minimum of stupidity? Who told him to be a perfectionist and go to such great excess and have a larger measure of stupidity? It is this striving for perfection in achieving the ultimate in stupidity that I cannot tolerate."

There is a popular adage, "If life gives you lemons, then make lemonade."

Rebbe Naftali would have agreed with this.

Chassidim of the old school had little use for anyone who flaunted his piety. What you are and what you do is between you and God. Manifesting a "holier than thou" attitude was soundly condemned.

As a young man, Rebbe Naftali of Ropsicz suspected that a certain very outwardly-pious Jew was less than genuine. He waited for an opportunity to test him, and this occurred once when there was overcrowding at the table and someone gave this man a shove.

"Take care!" Rebbe Naftali said to his colleagues. "You

must treat this man with respect. Why, this man is one who does penance by fasting every Monday and Thursday."

The man turned toward Rebbe Naftali, and with an angry voice said, "What do you mean every Monday and Thursday? Young man, I'll have you know that I fast all week, from *Shabbos* to *Shabbos*."

The man's abominable self-righteousness was thus exposed.

Just as chassidus taught us that impressing others with one's religiosity is despicable, it also taught that impressing *oneself* with one's own piety is spurious. Said Rebbe Naftali, "I prefer a *rasha* (sinner) who knows he is a *rasha*, to a *zaddik* who knows he is a *zaddik*."

Actually, this is taught by the Scriptures. Whereas the Torah says that the divine presence will rest among the Israelites even when they are not deserving(Leviticus XVI:6), it also says that a conceited person is abominable in the eyes of God (Proverbs XVI: 8).

⁂

Great-grandfather, the Rebbe of Hornostipol, had a large following of devotees. He suffered from a heart condition which ultimately ended his life in the early sixties.

One time, Great-grandfather developed a severe bout of hiccups, which stubbornly refused to respond to every known treatment. After three days of unabated hiccupping, it was feared that his heart might be affected, and he was advised to see a neurology professor in Kiev.

Accompanied by his attendant, who also served as interpreter since Great-grandfather knew little Russian, he went to Kiev. After completing the examination, the professor prescribed a radical treatment, namely, shocking the spinal cord by applying a red-hot poker to the spinal column.

The attendant interpreted the doctor's message, and Great-grandfather only said, "Nu," and stripped to the waist. The doctor put a poker into the fire, and after it reached a glowing heat, he ran it down the spinal column. Great-grandfather didn't budge nor emit a sound.

The doctor was bewildered. He saw the searing burn mark, yet the lack of any response made him think that the treatment did not "take." He reheated the poker, and applied it down the spinal column again, this time with greater pressure. Again, not a whimper, not a move.

The doctor thrust the poker onto the fireplace. "I cannot understand this!" he exclaimed. "This is not a human being; this is some kind of angel! The other day I had to perform this treatment on a robust, husky Cossack. I no sooner took the poker off the fire than he jumped out the second floor window. Here I have scorched this man twice and he does not even move a muscle!"

Great-grandfather asked the attendant, "What did the doctor say?" and the attendant translated the doctor's words.

Great-grandfather only sighed. "You know," he said, "when someone comes to me for help with a problem, and in spite of how much I wish to help him, I find myself unable to do so, and if at such a time I do not jump out the window, I certainly do not have to do so now."

❧

Ahavas yisroel, the love and devotion to a fellow Jew was always paramount.

We were told of the Rebbe of Sasov, who said that he had not understood what really constituted love of a fellow man until he learned it from a drunkard.

One time, the Rebbe of Sasov passed a tavern, and overheard a dialogue between two men well into their cups. One was professing how much he loved the other, but the other denied this was so.

"Ivan!" he cried. "Believe me when I tell you I love you more dearly than anything else in the world."

"Not so, Igor," Ivan replied. "You don't really love me."

Igor gulped down a glass of vodka. The tears streamed down his face. "I swear, Ivan, I love you with all my heart," he wept.

Ivan shook his head."No Igor,I don't believe that you love me. If you really do love me, tell me in what way I am hurting. Tell me what I am lacking. Tell me what my unsatisfied needs are."

The Rebbe of Sasov walked away. "Now I know," he said, "that unless I feel another person's pain, unless I know what his unmet needs are, I really have not achieved a feeling of love for him." *Ahavas yisroel* requires deep empathy to feel what the other person is lacking.

⁂

We heard many stories about *ahavas yisroel.* The Baal Shem Tov's greatest emphasis was on the overriding supremacy of *ahavas yisroel.*

Rebbe Elimelech once took upon himself two years of voluntary exile, so that the wandering and suffering would serve as expiation for his "sins" and elevate him to a higher level of spirituality.

At the termination of the exile, he returned home, and upon setting foot in his home town, he immediately inquired of the townfolk as to the welfare of his family. "We heard that your son, Eliezer, has been sick," someone said.

Rebbe Elimelech hastened to his home and burst in breathlessly. "How is the child?" he asked of his wife. "How is Eliezer?"

"Eliezer is fine, thank God," the wife answered. "He is playing with his friends."

"But I was told Eliezer was ill," Rebbe Elimelech said.

The wife shook her head. "No," she said, "Eliezer has not been sick." After a few moments pause she said, "Oh, I know what they meant. There is a neighbor who has a child named Eliezer, and yes, that Eliezer has been sick, but our Eliezer has, thank God, been well."

Rebbe Elimelech was relieved to hear that his son was well. But after a moment he said to himself, "So, Melech, Melech, that's how it is. It makes a difference to you whether it is *your* Eliezer or someone else's Eliezer that is sick? Then what have you accomplished with your exile? Back into exile, Melech. You still haven't changed." And thereupon, he bade his wife farewell and went back into exile for another year.

Is it possible for me to feel for another child the way I feel for my own? Probably not. But it is important to know that there were people who demanded of themselves this degree of *ahavas yisroel.*

❧

In psychiatric training, I learned a great deal about transference and countertransference, the latter being the attitudes of the therapist toward the patient and how it can affect the treatment.

Many decades before Freud, the Rebbe of Talna, after receiving supplicants all morning, was observed by his *gabbai* to be perspiring profusely. The latter expressed his surprise. All the Rebbe had done was to talk with people. Why should this have caused such intense sweating?

"All I did was talk?" the Rebbe replied. "Not so. You see, when someone comes to me with his problems and troubles, in order for me to truly grasp his situation, I must become him. I must shed my clothes and put on his. But after becoming him, I am as helpless as he, since I am now totally involved in his troubles. I must therefore become myself again. I must shed his clothes and put on my own again, in order to become an impartial outsider. Now with all the people I have seen this morning, and with each one, I must dress and undress, dress and undress. Can't you see how exhausting this is, and why I perspire so?"

Little wonder that the great chassidic masters were able to provide such great help to their followers. They knew the secret of countertransference, how to identify and how to detach.

❧

Father used to enjoy telling the following story of Rebbe Levi Yitzchok of Berdichev. In retrospect, I recall that he used to tell it on special occasions, especially at family *simchas* (joyous occasions) such as Bar Mitzvahs or weddings. I guess I was too dull to put two and two together at the time.

One Yom Kippur eve, the great Rebbe Levi Yitzchok appeared to be deepy worried. He had not begun the service, and several times called upon the congregants to say the *T'hilim* with greater fervor and to pray for mercy. His usual joyous expression had been replaced with features of anguish. He stood off in a corner, tearfully praying, obviously in great distress.

After a prolonged period, the Rebbe's countenance abruptly changed to one of jubiliation, and he began the Yom Kippur service with great joy. After the Yom Kippur services were completed, he addressed the congregation.

"The period between Rosh Hoshanah and Yom Kippur this year has been an exceedingly trying one for the people of Israel. The heavenly tribunal had come to a very stern judgment which would have exacted inordinate amounts of suffering from the Israelites. All the *zaddikim* had tried to intercede to try to overturn the decree, but their efforts had all been in vain. Faced with this terrible Divine wrath," said Rebbe Levi Yitzchok, "I was unable to begin the Yom Kippur service.

"In a nearby village," Rebbe Levi Yitzchok continued, "there lives a woman who was childless for many years after her marriage. Her prayers for a child had been unanswered until this past year, when she was blessed with a son. Needless to say, her whole world revolved around this child. She never let him out of her sight for a moment, and constantly attended to his needs.

"As Yom Kippur approached, it suddenly occurred to her that she would be unable to attend at *Kol Nidre* (the opening of the Yom Kippur service). She was in a terrible dilemma, for ever since her earliest years, she had never missed *Kol Nidre.* There was no way of getting anyone to watch the baby, because everyone, man, woman, and child in the village, would be at the synagogue.

Shortly before the beginning of the services, the baby fell asleep, and she anticipated that he would probably sleep for several hours. She thus decided that it would be safe for her to be away for the half hour or so to say the *Kol Nidre* at the synagogue.

During the *Kol Nidre* services, her thoughts began to run away with her. What if the baby did awaken and was crying? What if he moved about so much that he overturned the crib? Her imagination began to conjure the most frightening scenes of horror, and the moment the last word of *Kol Nidre* was uttered, the woman ran home in a frenzy, expecting to find the worst.

When she entered the house in a breathless panic, she found the infant peacefully and securely asleep in his crib. Overcome with relief, she turned her eyes to Heaven in gratitude. *Ribono Shel Olam* (Master of the Universe), she said, 'How can I ever thank you? I can only wish You that just as You have provided me with *nachas* from my child, so You should have *nachas* from Your children.'

"This perfect and sincere wish to the Almighty broke through all of the gates of Heaven and succeeded in overturning the evil decree," the Berdichever said.

I now know why Father told this story on special occasions. At those times when he experienced *nachas* from his children, he wished to share this blessing with all who joined in the celebration, that they should have *nachas* from their children, and, like the woman in the story, he wished the Almighty to have *nachas* from His children.

XI

Folk Tales

If it's the real thing, then it's the real thing; if you begin tampering with it . . . well, let the story speak for itself.

Yankel was a peasant who eked out his bare subsistence by delivering things, carrying heavy loads on his back. One time he delivered a package to a wealthy man, and happened to come in at mealtime when the man was enjoying a rich cheese omelet, deep-fried in butter. The sight of the omelet and the aroma made Yankel's mouth water.

On returning home, Yankel said to his wife, "Bella, the wealthy people sure know how to live. I just saw a cheese omelet, the likes of which I have never seen in my life. Oh, if only I could afford such a delicacy."

"Why can't you afford it?" Bella asked. "Just wait a few minutes and you will have a fine omelet."

Bella went into the kitchen, but since fresh eggs were far beyond their means, she took some flour and water and made a loose batter. Not having any butter, she poured the batter into a pan of hot oil, which had already been recycled several times. Finally, lacking cheese, she filled the "omelet" with mashed potatoes and set it before her eager husband.

Yankel dug into the "omelet" with great gusto, but after taking one bite of it, he spit it out. "Pfui!" said Yankel. "You know, Bella, these wealthy people are crazy. I don't know what in the world they see in these omelets that they consider them a delicacy."

Jewishness in its entirety is not only wholesome but actually delicious. The basic ingredients were dictated by God, with instructions to follow the recipes of those who prepared it: "Do not deviate from what they (the Torah authorities) tell you" (Deuteronomy XVII: 11).

But when the ingredients are changed, flour and water instead of eggs, mashed potatoes instead of cheese, and recycled oil instead of butter, isn't it obvious that it is no longer palatable?

Those who have tampered with the recipe are coming to discover more and more that their dish is not tasty. People are not satisfied with a religion that they can mold to their hearts' content. They recognize that the will of God ceases to be just that when that will is determined by a majority vote of a congregation's membership.

The latter have become alarmed by the t'shuva movement. Rightly so. Once one tastes a rich omelet, he will never accept an ersatz.

A great deal of wisdom has been preserved in folk tales which have been transmitted through the generations.

The collection of stories of the "wise men" of Chelm offers many amusing tales. Some of these are laden with profound wisdom.

Modern psychology has a great deal to say about identity problems. There is the search for identity, the identity crisis, the pathologic identity, and various others. Because identity is so vital to the personality, many people in search of an identity because of a feeling of internal emptiness will pursue the acquisition of some type of label, whether this be a professional title, an office position, or distinction by wealth and property. Too often the fragile and transitory nature of an external identity is not appreciated.

It is told that one of the wise men of Chelm found himself in a predicament in the public bath house, because without the distinction of clothes, everyone looked essentially alike. "Among all these men who look alike," he thought, "how will I ever know which one is me?"

A brilliant idea then occurred to him. He took a piece of red string and tied it around his great toe. Now he was distinctly different and would not lose himself among all the bathers.

Unfortunately, in the process of sudsing and showering, the red string came loose and fell off. One of the other bathers happened to step on it in such a fashion that the string became wrapped around his great toe.

After a while, the wise man happened to notice the string bearer, and looking down at his own foot, saw nothing. He was a bit befuddled, and then walked up to the man wearing the red string.

"Perhaps you can help me," he said. "It is clear to me who *you* are. But tell me, who am *I*?"

It should be apparent that the current psychologic preoccupation with the search for identity betrays the fact that many people feel very poor in self esteem. People who have a good sense of self have no identity problem. The correct approach to resolving identity problems is thus to gain a correct sense of oneself. Invariably, the poor self-esteem is a result of a distorted self-concept.

Too many people, instead of correcting the mistaken self perception and thereby dealing effectively with the roots of this problem, seek to attain a sense of self from external sources. It is as though they are saying, "I cannot tolerate being a nobody. If I become a doctor, then I will be a somebody. If I have a luxurious home or a fancy automobile in my driveway, then I will be a somebody. If I marry into a prominent family, or if I am given the honor of the first *hakafah* on Simchat Torah (marching with the Torah around the reader's pulpit), or if my picture appears in the newspaper standing near a prominent official, then I will be a somebody."

As the Chelm story demonstrates so clearly, external identities are unreliable and transitory. In the first place, I am never really *myself*. If my only claim to an identity is being a doctor or lawyer, then I share this identity with hundreds of thousands of other people, but have none which is truly my own. If my identity is the luxurious home or automobile, then it goes along with the title to the house or car. Like the red string, if the house or the car is lost, the identity goes with it.

It is tragic that people look elsewhere for identities. We all have adequate ingredients in ourselves to fashion a fine identity. We need only to discover and develop them.

❧

Father's advice was widely sought. He had an uncanny capacity for working out satisfactory solutions to seemingly insoluble problems. Judges would often recommend that the litigants take their cases to Father for out-of-court settlement. Father received a citation from the Milwaukee judiciary for his contributions in resolving difficult cases.

Yet there were some who would reject Father's advice. Father would say, "Sometimes I would rather that people would *not* listen to me, because then they would realize I was right. When they follow my instructions and all goes well, they are apt to think, 'Had I done it *my* way, things would have been better yet.' But it is when they do not listen to me that they really appreciate my advice."

Although Father had considerable persuasive powers, he sometimes encountered a stonewall of obstinacy, when someone just remained obstinate and refused to accept logic. At times like this, Father would tell the following story.

In the early days of the railroad, villagers in the back country heard of a miraculous new invention, an engine that could actually pull many wagons. This appeared incredible, because for thousands of years, in fact since man could remember, the only way to get a wagon to move was to hitch it up to horses or mules. Now here was a wagon that could move without horses! Unbelievable! They decided to send a representative to the big city through which the locomotive travelled, to personally investigate this phenomenon and report to them whether this was indeed true, and if so, how such a marvelous thing operated.

The representative visited the big city, and upon his return, called a town meeting. Yes, it was true. He had seen with his very own eyes this huge machine on wheels which could pull several carriages without the use of horses. But this was not accomplished by any sorcery whatsoever. In fact, it was very understandable.

The representative then drew a picture of the steam engine, and pointed out the principle of its operation, that when water was heated to steam in a closed container, it produced a great force which was then exerted upon a piston. This piston then pushed a lever which was attached to a wheel at an eccentric angle, moving the wheel and consequently the whole locomotive. It was all perfectly understandable.

A few of the villagers nodded affirmatively. Some scratched their heads in wonderment and disbelief. The representative then repeated the explanation to the satisfaction of all attending. All but one, that is.

One villager protested. "This is foolishness," he said. "There is no way that a carriage can travel without horses. We know that, our fathers knew that, as did their ancestors before them. Now this man who claims to have seen otherwise was somehow bewitched into thinking he saw a carriage move without horses, and you all believe him!"

The villagers rose to the defense of the representative. "This is not witchcraft, " they said. "The mechanism of the engine is fully understandable." Each in his own way then explained the way the engine worked, and the representative again drew diagrams and explained every little detail, until finally the skeptic conceded that the phenomenon was real, and affirmed that he too understood how the steam engine worked.

All the villagers heaved a sign of relief, and sat back to relax. The representative then asked if there were any remaining questions that anyone wished to raise.

The lone skeptic stood up. "I understand everything you have said," he stated, "and your diagrams are very clear. There is only one question that still bothers me. Where, on that contraption that you drew, just where do you attach the horses?"

❧

One of the stories of the wise men of Chelm was just another amusing story until I became involved in dealing with government bureaucracy, at which time I marvelled at the story's prophetic foresight.

The story goes that one winter night in Chelm, there fell a blanket of snow so clean and smooth, that when the elders of the city arose in the early hours of the morning, they were overcome by its pristine beauty. But they then realized that it was the practice of the *shamas* (beadle) to go from house to house, knocking on the doors and arousing the worshippers to come to morning services. With his great big klutzy feet, the *shamas* would trample and ruin this lovely and beautiful snow. That must not be allowed to happen!

The wise men of Chelm gathered into emergency session, and after a great deal of deliberation, came up with a solution which would be approached and almost equalled by the efficiency of modern government bureaucracy. To prevent the *shamas* from trampling the smooth snow with his big feet, *four men would carry the shamas from door to door.*

❧

There have been times when I have been called upon to render an opinion on a thorny ethical issue. At times I have found myself in a dilemma, and I have been better able to explain my position, thanks to a story which I had often heard from Father.

There was once a young girl who was very devout. One time she fell ill, and her condition became critical. A specialist who examined her said that there was only one thing which could save her life, and that was an ingredient which was found only in a hog's liver. The girl had to eat hog liver if she were to survive.

The girl refused, saying that there was no way that she would eat *trefa*. The girl's father brought the local rabbi to talk with her, and the rabbi informed the girl that when there was danger to life, the laws of *kashrut* were suspended. Furthermore, she was not only permitted, but also obligated by the law of the Torah to do whatever was necessary to save her life. In short, the rabbi said, in this case the Torah demanded of her that she eat hog liver.

The girl reluctantly consented, but stated that she would eat hog liver only if the animal were ritually slaughtered. Bad enough that she had to eat *chazer* (pork), she said, but she is not going to eat *n'velah* (meat that was not ritually slaughtered) on top of it.

The rabbi tried to explain that there is no such thing as ritual slaughter of the hog, but all his arguing was in vain. Either there would be ritual slaughter or she would not eat.

The distraught father went to the *shochet* (abbatoir) and explained his plight. He knew it was absurd, he said, but the child is deathly sick and cannot be reasoned with. Would the *shochet* please have mercy on his sick child and slaughter the hog for him?

The *shochet* shrugged his shoulders. This was the craziest thing he had ever heard of, but there was no point in delaying the cure. So the *shochet* went ahead and performed a ritual slaughter.

The girl was not yet satisfied. She wanted the animal's lungs inspected according to *halacha* to make certain that there was no lesion that would render it *trefa*. Bad enough that she had to eat *chazer*, she said, but a double *trefa* is worse than a single *trefa*.

Since there was no reasoning with her, the *shochet*

removed the hog's lungs for inspection, and as luck would have it, there was a questionable lesion. The *shochet* took the lung to the rabbi for a decision.

The rabbi examined the lung and said, "If this lesion were in the lung of a cow, it would not pose a problem, because it is not *per se* a *trefa* lesion. But how in the world can I rule that a *chazer* is kosher?"

Western civilization has gone wild with the sanction of "redeeming features." Many things which are patently objectionable are being accorded social approval because of "redeeming features."

There is no doubt in anyone's mind that television has resulted in the introduction of very explicit degenerate behavior into the living rooms of many homes, and indiscriminately to many young and impressionable children. Yet, television is considered "kosher" because of its newscasts (of questionable value) and its educational programs. Some people engage in shady business practices, but donate some of their profits to worthy causes. Frank violations of religious statutes may be perpetuated by individuals who are the economic pillars of the congregation. Everything is apt to be rendered acceptable because of some "redeeming feature."

It would be well to know that no matter what the considerations may be, *chazer* simply cannot be deemed kosher.

❧

I received my rabbinic education in terms of theory at the yeshiva, but I had a lesson in practical rabbinics from Malka.

Malka was from the old school. No question but that after Malka was fashioned, they threw the mold away. There will never be another Malka.

Malka was lucid until her last day. She stopped counting her age after reaching one hundred. She lived with her daughter until the *latter* entered the home for the aged. Malka had to enter the institution together with her daughter.

Malka was a wise woman with a heart of gold and a tongue as sharp as a razor. No one dared cross Malka.

When I gave my first eulogy as a fledgling rabbi , Malka was in the audience. I felt I had delivered an excellent homily, but after the service was over, Malka called me aside.

"Sonny," she said. (Only Malka could call the rabbi "Sonny." After all, she was old enough to have been my great-grandmother.) "Sonny," Malka said, "the deep wisdom of the Talmud and all the philosophy is for *you* to know. When you give the eulogy, you should say how the children were very respectful, loving, and devoted to their mother."

"Respectful and loving?" I challenged. "Malka, this woman, who was a pious and kosher-observant woman all of her life had to spend her last two years in a *trefa* nursing home because her six well-to-do children did not make the effort to have her cared for at her home, although it was completely realistic and feasible. You call that respectful and devoted?"

Malka shook her head. "Sonny, you are telling Malka something she doesn't know? Maybe you are more learned than Malka, but Malka has been around a bit. You listen to Malka, Sonny.

"The interpretation of the Talmud is very fine, but except in a study class, it doesn't make anyone feel any better. The lady who died, you can't help any more. But if you say about the children like Malka tells you to, then it makes the children feel better." Then, winking at me, she added, "And it wouldn't hurt the congregation either.

"Now when the great day comes for Malka, then you can say what you wish. But please speak in Yiddish so that I can understand."

⸙

I can remember Mrs. Glass for as long as I can remember myself.

Mrs. Glass was very active in the *shul* ladies' auxiliary, and was a frequent visitor at our home when I was a child. She always had chewing gum for me.

Many years later, when I was an intern at Mount Sinai Hospital, Mrs. Glass was admitted on transfer from the home for the aged because of pneumonia. She was deep into her eighties, and had lost both legs due to diabetes.

I was called to administer an intravenous antibiotic to her. In order to reassure her, I said, "This needle will only give you a tiny sting. It won't hurt much."

"Foolish child," Mrs. Glass said. "Let it hurt! Do you think a person wants to leave a world that is pleasant?"

I have many times recalled Mrs. Glass's words, especially when dealing with geriatric patients, some of whom appear to be chronically dissatisfied with whatever is done for them. It can be most frustrating, when you minister to elderly patients in whatever capacity, and feel that your efforts are unappreciated.

I have shared Mrs. Glass's message with many workers in geriatrics. Elderly people's complaints do not always mean that their actual needs have been unmet, or that they are really displeased with what you have done for them. Sometimes their dissatisfaction is defensive, and should not be taken to mean that they are unappreciative.

If you go on a vacation and it nears its end, and you have to return home to the drudgery and burden of everyday life, the kindest thing that can happen is for the weather to be perfectly miserable the last two days. This way it is much easier to go back than if the weather were ideal for golfing or fishing up to the very last day.

When the time of departure from this world draws near, it is so much easier to take leave if the world is perceived as a rather uncomfortable place anyway.

❧

I was always intrigued by philosophy. When I began to read the work of contemporary thinkers, however, I often found myself stymied. I would often reread a passage numerous times, yet find myself unable to grasp its content. I would listen to philosophers discuss things in which they used the words and phrases that I had encountered in my readings, but alas, I had no idea what they were talking about. Could it be that I was not a philosopher after all?

The same thing happened with my exposure to psychoanalysis. Freud's writings were clear and lucid, whether I agreed with all of his points or not. But some of the later psychoanalysts seemed to be producing highly sophisticated confusion. It bothered me that after considering myself knowledgeable in psychoanalysis, I had to deal with my inability to comprehend.

I then remembered a story my father had told. Boruch Yossel used to travel from time to time to various cities on business matters. Boruch Yossel was a pious Jew, his father having been a *shochet*, but he did not have much claim to brilliance.

One time while en route, Boruch Yossel spent the night at an inn. After he had retired, a priest came to the inn for lodging, and was given the other bed in Boruch Yossel's room.

Boruch Yossel arose before dawn, since he had to get started on his journey very early. He groped in the dark for his clothes and suitcase, but happened to reach the priest's garb and case rather than his own.

While Boruch Yossel was waiting for his train at the station, he happened to pass by a mirror and he was stunned. "What in the world am I doing wearing the clothes of a priest?" he thought. "I am not a priest! I am a Jew, Boruch Yossel!"

He turned around and looked into the mirror again. There it was, and there was no denying it. "There must be some mistake," he thought. "Yet I cannot deny the testimony of my senses. The garb is definitely that of a priest."

Suddenly he thought of a solution to his bewilderment. "Let me open my suitcase," he said to himself. "If it contains a *talis* and *tfillin*, then I am Boruch Yossel. If it contains the accoutrements of the mass, then I am a priest."

Of course, since he had mistakenly taken the priest's suitcase, Boruch Yossel found all the priestly paraphernalia. "That appeared to be conclusive. I must be a priest after all."

But his mind could not rest. "How can I be a priest when I know myself to be Boruch Yossel, the *shochet's* son, and when I have a wife, Zelda Chaya, and seven children, they should live and be well?"

So Boruch Yossel was again plunged into the question of his true identity. Then he had a bright idea which he felt would resolve the question once and for all. "Let me open this Latin Bible," he reasoned. "If I can understand what it says, then I must be a priest. For how would Boruch Yossel, the *shochet's* son, know Latin? If, however, I do not understand it, then for certain I am Boruch Yossel."

He then opened the Bible, and of course, could not understand a single word. "There," he said, "that proves it beyond any doubt. I do not understand a word of this, so clearly I cannot be a priest."

But just as he was enjoying the certainty of his identity, his eyes again met the mirror, and once more he saw himself in priestly regalia. Now there is just no way that any logical argument can overcome the testimony of one's senses. Is it not universally accepted that seeing is believing? "I see I am a priest," Boruch Yossel said. "There is just no way that I can escape that conclusion."

But Boruch Yossel was tormented by the fact that he could not understand any of the Latin Bible. "How is it that I can be a priest and not understand the Latin Bible?"

But as repeated confrontations with the mirror reinforced his identity as a priest, Boruch Yossel was left with only one explanation. "The undeniable and irrefutable fact is that I *am* a priest," he said. "But as far as my not understanding the Bible," he reasoned, "that is no objection. It's just that all other priests do not understand the Latin Bible either."

And so, I came to Boruch Yossel's conclusion. True, I did not understand contemporary philosophy and some of the later psychoanalysts, but that was not inconsistent with my being a philosopher or psychoanalyst. For, you see, none of the contemporary philosophers or psychoanalysts really understand any of their works either.

When I trained to become a psychiatrist, I learned a great deal about Freudian psychology. At that time, psychoanalysis as a method of treatment was popular. On a visit with Father, I explained some of the theory of psychoanalytic treatment, and that a course of treatment might take several years before results were evident.

It was obvious from Father's reaction that he did not think too highly of a treatment that could not produce results for several years. He then told me the following story.

One of the nobility in feudal Russia was a man who was of benign nature, and did not participate in pogroms. The more fervent anti-Semites in his community tried to incite him against the Jews, but were unable to persuade him.

This nobleman had a pet dog of whom he was extremely fond. It then occurred to one of the anti-Semites to exploit this love for the dog.

"Your Excellency," he said to the nobleman, "you have been very tolerant and kind to the Jews in your domain. You must know, however, that they are an ungrateful people, and do not appreciate the protection you grant them.

"You know how clever those Jews are. Why, they know how to teach a dog how to talk. They could teach your dog to talk, Your Excellency, but they will not do so because you are not one of them, because you are a gentile.

"Oh, they will never admit this to you, Your Excellency. They will deny that they have this skill, and will give you thousands of reasons why it cannot be done. Believe me, Your Excellency, I have seen them do it. If they refuse you, it is only because you are a gentile. They are utterly unappreciative of your benevolence."

This time he struck in a vulnerable spot. The nobleman's fondness of his dog was so great that his emotions overcame all rationality. He sent for the leaders of the Jewish community.

"You are well aware," he said, "that you have had uninterrupted peace and prosperity in my fiefdom, as has not been enjoyed by Jews elsewhere in the land. In return for my protection, I make only one request of you. My dog is my constant companion, and is very dear to me. It would give me great pleasure to converse with my dog. I know that you possess the secret of teaching a dog to speak, and I wish you to do this favor for me."

"Certainly you jest, Your Excellency," the Jews replied. "We cannot teach a dog to speak. No one has ever taught a dog to speak. That is absurd."

The nobleman became angry. "Aha, so that's how it is! That is how you Jews show your gratitude! You refuse to teach my dog to speak because I am a gentile."

No amount of protestation or explanation was of any avail. The nobleman grew progressively more irate. He was adamant, and finally decreed that the Jews had 30 days to teach the dog to speak, and if they persisted in their refusal, they would face banishment or the wrath of a pogrom.

The bewildered Jews were beside themselves. How do you deal with such irrationality? They called community meetings, prayed fervently, and decreed days of fasting and penitence. As the end of the 30-day period approached, they began loading their belongings on wagons to leave the area and escape from the inevitable pogrom.

On the last day of the grace period, a humble tailor, one of the lesser luminaries of the community, arose to speak to the congregation. "My people," he said, "you have exhausted all of your means. I ask your permission to intercede with the nobleman."

"You!" they exclaimed. "What do you think you can accomplish? All the rabbis and scholars have not been able to overcome his delusions. What can you do?"

"What do you have to lose?" the tailor asked. "You already have prepared to leave tomorrow. Your wagons are all loaded."

The community agreed that there was nothing to lose, and the little tailor took off for the palace. A short while later, he returned, with the dog on a leash. Triumphantly he exclaimed, "Unload the wagons, everyone. We are staying!"

"What do you mean, 'we are staying,'?" they asked. "And what on earth are you doing with the nobelman's dog?"

The tailor shrugged. "I simply told him that I would teach the dog how to talk. But I explained to him that even a human being, who is so much more intelligent than a dog, does not learn how to speak in a short time. Why, it takes a child at least two years to speak well, and for a dog, it would take at least four years."

"Are you mad?" they asked the tailor. "What do you plan to do after four years?"

"Relax, my friends," the tailor said. "Four years is a long time. During the four years, something is guaranteed to happen that will get us off the hook. Perhaps the nobleman will die in that interval. Perhaps I will die, or perhaps the dog will die. Four years is a long time."

"You see," Father said, "any treatment that takes so long a time is bound to coincide with some changes in the patient's life. He may marry. He may divorce. He may make money, he may lose money. He may have a child, or perhaps a grandchild. The variables that can occur in a four-year period are legion. How can one attribute any change to the treatment?"

I never did become a psychoanalyst.

❧

When I learned in psychiatry that Sigmund Freud had described the "repetition compulsion" phenomenon, wherein some people appear to be compelled to repeat the same pathological behavior time after time regardless of its consequences, I recalled a story I had heard Father tell when I was a child. At that time, I thought it was just a funny story, only to learn much later that it was a lesson in psychology.

In the days of the horse-drawn taxi, a traveller arrived at a train station and hired a cab. After giving the driver his destination, he cautioned him, "Please avoid this particular road. There is a deep ditch there."

The driver started the horses. "Just sit back and relax, my friend," he said. "Don't worry. I have been driving these roads for thirty-five years."

As they proceeded on the passenger said, "I can see the way you are heading. Please don't go that way. The road there has that big pit."

The driver smiled reassuringly. "No need to fear," he said. "I have been driving these roads for thirty-five years."

Soon they turned off onto a path. The passenger hollered, "Hey! This is the path I told you to avoid. It has this great big ditch ahead."

"Quit fretting," the driver said. "Haven't I told you? I have been driving these roads for thirty-five years."

Before long they reached the ditch and fell in, wagon, horse, and passenger. The driver crawled out from beneath the wreckage. "Funny thing, I swear," he said. "I have been driving these roads for thirty-five years, and every time I pass here, this is what always happens."

❧

After many years of psychiatric practice, I began to realize that while some people's problems are due to episodes of illness, whether neurosis or psychosis, other people have characterologic problems. That is, they have a certain behavior pattern which is part of their personalities, rather than being an episodic change in their mental state. I have found the latter to be very resistant to change, and even when a person asserts that he has changed his character, the change is apt to be superficial at best.

It should not have taken me so long to grasp this if I had understood a story Father used to tell.

Zurach was a tightwad. He was the kind of man who if challenged with "your money or your life," would probably have carefully weighed both options.

One day Zurach came into *shul* with obviously conflicting feelings. He was announcing a mazel tov because his wife had given birth to a son. But he knew he would have to invite guests to the *bris* (circumcision). "I guess I will have to serve refreshments," he lamented.

"Refreshments?" his friend asked. "At a *bris*? Zurach, you must be joking. At a *bris*, you don't serve refreshments. You must provide a full feast, with fish, meat, wine, and spirits. And you know what else, Zurach? You are going to have to provide even more food for your guests than anyone else. It is just a fact of human nature that when the host is miserly and begrudges the food, it stimulates the guests' appetites, and they eat twice as much."

Zurach had no choice but to serve a full dinner at the *bris.* While the guests were enjoying the meal, Zurach ran over to his friend and cried, "Hey, look, I don't begrudge them anything. They can gladly eat as much as they want, I swear it. But it isn't helping at all. They are still eating too much."

❧

Father used to tell a story which helped me realize that the absurdity of the bureaucracy is not a totally new phenomenon. Nonsensical regulations have been around for a long time.

It seems that a widow, who lived in a small Russian village, had a son who emigrated to America. Month after month went by without a single word from him, and as the months turned into years, she began to fear that some evil had befallen him. One day a traveller came through the village and told her that he had met her son in Chicago, and gave her the address where the latter could be contacted.

Since the woman was unable to write, she hurried off to the village scribe who performed such functions for the illiterate population. She dictated a letter full of anguish and hurt. "Why have you not written to me in three years? I did not know what to think. After not hearing from you for so long, I began to fear the worst," and so on.

After the dictation was complete, she asked the scribe to read the letter to her.

The scribe began, "Dear Son, I have received your most welcome letter and was just delighted to hear from you . . ." The woman interrupted, "No! What are you saying? That is not true. I haven't heard a word from him in three years!"

The scribe shook his head, "Sorry, lady," he said, "that is

the form we use. That is what the beginning of every letter we write must say."

The wisdom of Solomon is again affirmed. "There is nothing new under the sun" (Ecclesiastes I: 9).

XII

Memories Of the Old Timers

I was privileged to know many colorful people.

The generation of eastern European immigrants is a historical phenomenon that will never be repeated. Fortunately, some writers who described the lower East Side of New York in the early nineteen hundreds have preserved some of these induplicable characters for posterity.

In the back of the *shul*, in Milwaukee, there was a little room with a table,chairs, a stove and a sink. Before *Mincha* or on a Sunday morning, the old-timers would sit around drinking tea and sharing stories. Progress had replaced the brass samovar with the tea kettle, although we did have a samovar as a decorative piece. Glass after glass of tea was gulped down, in quantities and at a temperature which defies human physiology according to medical science.

I used to sit with the men who sometimes recited the events of the day, which generally related to their gathering of *shmatas*, paper, scrap iron, and old clothes. At other times they would reminisce, and one of my favorite events was when they tried to outdo each other, such as who had come to America first. The measuring stick was how many reigning presidents of the United States one had survived. Even prior to learning history at school, I became well familiar with presidential history, as the old-timers vied for the distinction of who had buried the most presidents. Some had come to America during the reign of Taft, almost all had been here under Woodrow Wilson, Harding and Coolidge. Ruben and a few others had found Teddy Roosevelt in office. But when old man Rachmiel would walk in, all fell silent. Rachmiel had come to the U.S. in 1896, and he had buried McKinley! This was a distinction no one else could claim, and Rachmiel took great pride in his seniority.

Many had nicknames, each of which had a story behind its acquisition. I never knew Chaim's real last name; he was called "Chaim from America." One was called *"Yom Hashishi,"* (the sixth day) after the opeing words of the Friday night *kiddush*. They used to tell about a man who sat up as he was being carried to his grave during his funeral, and then lived on for some twenty years afterward, known to everyone as *"Shmulik der Toiter,"* (the dead Samuel).

These people were interesting, inspiring, and often very amusing. The English language was never the same again after falling into their hands. Leo Rosten so beautifully immortalized Hyman Kaplan. I knew many Hyman Kaplans.

The women would often talk about their physical aches and pains, and one related how the doctor had given her "an epidemic" (hypodermic) in the arm. Another had suffered from a "blood clock," and yet another had sustained a broken "blood whistle." During World War II, the dousing of all lights at night was a "blow-out" (blackout).

Their invectives were, "Sharrrrup!" or "Gerrorrorreer!" (get out of here). One of the worst expletives was "Gey in die

Hell arhein!"

Their accounts of how they had become naturalized U.S. citizens were often hilarious. Moshe insisted he was a citizen of the "nineteen States." ("Nineteen" was as close as he could get to "United.") Another would tell of how he had been carefully coached to give correct answers to questions he did not understand, but got into difficulty when the judge reversed the sequence of his interrogation, and asked for the number of times Motel had been married *before* inquiring about his age, receiving the amazing reply, "sixty-six." Another, when asked by the judge who the first president was, promptly and proudly responded, "Berl Forman," who had indeed been the first president of the Russian *shul* on Garfield Avenue. This was clearly more relevant to him than dear old George Washington.

When I brought home Rosten's masterpiece, Hyman Kaplan became a kind of hero for my father. He shared Kaplan's shrewd reasoning and his refusal to surrender to arbitrary and often illogical laws of grammar.

These were individuals in the true sense of the word. Each was a character in his own right, fiercely individualistic. All of these first generation Americans were distinct and unique, and each had a mind of his own.

Perhaps this is the pseudo-reality of nostalgia, yet, I hardly see many such individuals any more. Most people today are the product of schools and colleges, which have molded them into nearly identical persons, like so many tin soldiers. Mass-production industry has turned out millions of look-alike automobiles, and mass education has produced millions of think-alike people. Whatever bit of individualism might have survived the educational system has been brought into conformity by the cudgel of the mass media. Sometimes, flying over a modern suburb, I see rows and rows of houses, all alike. I even wonder, how does one ever know where he lives? And in these identical houses live identical people. How boring!

The old timers were all unique. Even if the diversity occasionally gave rise to some disunity, it was nevertheless refreshing.

A frequent finding among these first generation immigrants was their insistence on providing their children with all that they had lacked. Having been deprived of secular education by both poverty and repressive anti-Semitic laws in Russia, they utilized the blessings and freedom of the land of opportunity to their fullest. They emphasized the importance of education, and sacrificed to see their children through college. And so it was that the pushcart peddlers, small delicatessen and grocery store proprietors, and sweat shop workers became the fathers of some of the country's foremost scientists, doctors, lawyers, and economists.

The tragedy was that in their enthusiasm to give their children what they lacked, they neglected to give them what they *had:* the precious heritage of Jewish education. So engrossed with the new opportunities America could provide for their children, they allowed Jewish education to be a distant second in importance, relegated to a few hours a week in an after-school-hours Talmud Torah.

⁂

"Der alter Shye" (old man Isaiah) was the way I knew him, because that was what everyone called him.

How old was Shye? No one knew for certain, but it was

common knowledge that he was over one hundred. Do you know how much a hundred is to a child? It is the greatest number in the world. I stood in awe of someone who was *one hundred* years old.

Shye did not worship in Father's *shul*, but I would see him when we went to the Beth Medrosh Hagodol synagogue on special occasions.

One Rosh Hoshanah my brother went to the Beth Medrosh Hagodol to blow the *shofar* for the congregation, and I accompanied him. There was the alter Shye, walking up and down the aisle, wearing his *talis* and holding a closed prayer book in hand with one finger stuck in between the pages.

I observed that during the entire service, Shye paced up and down the long aisle, occasionally stopping at the *bimah* (pulpit) to take a pinch of snuff from the snuff box. (Incidentally, I still am uneasy in a *shul* that does not have a snuff box on the *bimah*. To me, this is an integral accoutrement of the *shul*, and the latter is incomplete without it. Furthermore, the snuff box provided an opportunity for *gemilas chesed* (acts of benevolence). Someone was always walking around offering a pinch of snuff to the congregants.) However, Shye's lips never moved. Shye wasn't *davening*!

A seven-year-old knows no protocol, and I didn't think that there was anything wrong with my approaching him. I simply went over and asked Shye, "How come you don't *daven* like you are supposed to?"

The old man pointed a scolding finger at me. "Listen here, son," he said. "I wish you too should *daven* for ninety-six years like I did, and then you can quit, too. Enough is enough!"

Well, I started *davening* at six or seven. If der alter Shye's blessing comes true, I can quit at one hundred three.

⸙

The following anecdote is a perfectly useless bit of trivia, which I record only for the benefit of some future chronicler of the Jewish community of Milwaukee, who might otherwise not have access to this little historical item.

There is a Jewish cemetery in Milwaukee known as the Second Home Cemetery. One might think that the title was aptly as well as poetically chosen to designate man's eternal abode. That is not quite how the name was selected.

The first generation immigrants who founded the Litvishe *shul* had acquired this plot of land for a cemetery. On the way there, they passed a nearby cemetery entitled Forest Home Cemetery. Their English being somewhat less than perfect, they misread the title as "*First* Home Cemetery," and reasoned that if this other place were called "*First* Home," then their cemetery should be called "*Second* Home."

As I said, a total useless bit of data, but since this may not have been recorded elsewhere, I feel that this should not be lost to posterity.

⸙

Old Eliezer lived to be eighty-eight, and had celebrated his sixtieth wedding anniversary. He had made the rather common progression from carrying bundles of rags on his back, to a pushcart, to the luxury of a horse and wagon, and finally to a small corner grocery. He was a happy man, and lived a full life. He was always at *shul* morning and evening, and joined all the study classes on *Shabbos*.

When Eliezer died, he left his *sukka* to me as a bequest. (Apparently, his children had no use for it.) It consisted of a few pieces of lumber, enough to construct a five-by-five foot hut, and a few poles upon which the corn husks could be laid, to commemorate the temporary dwellings of our ancestors on their exodus from the enslavement in ancient Egypt. Every year Eliezer had put together this little hut with love and devotion. Perhaps he had also remembered the teaching of the Rabbis, that the *sukka*, a temporary dwelling, is symbolic of the transitory dwelling of man on this physical planet, and that the seven or eight days spent in this hut during the Sukkos festival corresponds to man's seven or eight decades of sojourn on earth, during which he has the opportunity to prepare for his permanent residence.

Eliezer's son, Martin, benefited from the education and freedom of enterprise in this land. He became quite wealthy, and acquired a winter home in Florida, to which he drove in his luxurious Cadillac. He was too busy and successful to be in *shul* morning and evening, or join in the *Shabbos* study groups. With two lavish homes he had no need for the makeshift *sukka*. He went through two marriages and several coronaries, dying at the age of fifty-three.

Martin's brother was a successful attorney. He drank too much, had a ruinous marriage, and died in his fifties.

Family histories such as these were not uncommon. Blinded by the opportunities they could give their children in this new land, and in their zeal to provide them with all that they had lacked, the immigrants to this country often failed to give their children what they *did* have: the secret that could make life meaningful and hardship tolerable, without which even material comforts and abundance were void and depressing.

❧

Our home was frequently visited by itinerant rabbis. Many of these solicited on behalf of yeshivos and benevolent institutions, both here and in the Holy Land. Others, who had fallen on bad times, solicited for themselves.

The lot of the itinerant rabbis was not an enviable one. They travelled from city to city, lodging in less than comfortable accommodations, often in a community hospice. They were often referred to with the uncomplimentary appellation "schnorrers," an insult which they did not deserve.

Some were most interesting characters. There was Reb Meir Shye, who never spoke from sundown Friday until Saturday night, to avoid the possibility of desecrating the sacred *Shabbos* by talk which was unbecoming. Except for the prayers or his Torah study, Reb Meir Shye communicated by sign language during all of the *Shabbos*.

Then there was Reb Hershe, who as a young child had the good fortune to meet our great-great-grandfather, the Rebbe of Sanz. Reb Hershe had voluntarily restricted himself from eating any dairy products or meat foods outside of his own home. In those days, supervised kosher milk was a scarcity, as was kosher meat that met his scrupulous standards. In all of his travels, he lived on fish and vegetables.

Reb Hershe stayed at our home several weeks each year, and Mother let him prepare his own foods in our kitchen. Although the strict standard of kosher laws observed in our home could hardly be exceeded, Reb Hershe's restrictions were respected.

I learned from this that just because some people may exercise greater restrictions or observances than yourself, you do not have to be critical of them as being "fanatic," or accuse them of having a "holier-than-thou" attitude. Reb Hershe was welcome in our home every year, even though his presence did cause some inconvenience.

All of the itinerant rabbis had stories to tell. Many told of Jerusalem, of the sacred places in the Holy Land, and of wondrous deeds of the sages there. All were well-travelled, and I learned more about American and world geography from the itinerant rabbis than I ever did in school.

After an exhausting day of door-to-door soliciting, undoubtedly having some doors slammed in their faces, they would come to our *shul* and home and unwind. Some played chess with me, and others questioned me on what I had learned in Torah that week. Many had comments to make about the portion of the Torah that I had learned. Some were chassidim who had visited either of my grandfathers in Europe, and would tell of their contacts with them.

The rabbis would often join the tea-drinkers in the kitchen of the shul. They would unburden themselves to listeners. Several had their families in Europe, and were soliciting funds to enable them to bring their families to America. They would tell of the events of the day, how some people received them warmly, and invited them for a cup of coffee, and occasionally how some would send them flying. I used to listen to their conversations, and they provided me with a measure of understanding of the variations in human nature.

How wisely does the Talmud stress the *mitzvah* of

providing food and shelter to wanderers. "Let the poor be frequent visitors in your home" (Ethics of the Fathers I: 5). Like every other *mitzvah*, the benefits far exceed the effort expended.

❧

I knew some interesting couples.

You must realize that in the old country, marriages were often arranged. Parents would decide that their children would marry one another, and that was all there was to it. Courtship was non-existent. Frequently, the couple were introduced to each other at the wedding ceremony.

Surprisingly, or perhaps not so surprisingly, the majority of these marriages worked out well. Firstly, this method eliminated the distorting and misleading influence of infatuation, wherein passion renders people oblivious to gross incompatibilities. Parents who knew their children well and were devoted to them were in a position to make a choice free of the impact of physical attraction. People married within their faith and generally within their socio-economic groups. Many sources of domestic strife were thus eliminated.

Secondly, marriage was assumed to be primarily and essentially for the purpose of procreating and raising a family. The passion and romance advocated by Hollywood as principal features of a man-woman relationship were nowhere to be seen. These kinds of purpose and goal undoubtedly permitted young men and women to learn to know one another and adjust to each other in a lasting relationship. The knowledge that one was to share one's life with the other partner led to looking for and discovering things in the other partner which would make one's life pleasant and enable the marriage to achieve its goal.

Yet there were some strange pairings that came out of this system. Benzy and Esther were a couple who celebrated their sixty-fifth anniversary. I don't think there was a day in their married lives that Esther did not heap a pile of invectives on Benzy's head. If she would run out of curses in her repertoire, she would invent new ones. Yet together they enjoyed their children, grandchildren, and their many great-grandchildren.

Esther had set herself a goal of reciting the *kedusha* (the glorification of God by the angels) once daily for *each* grandchild. This was Esther's own invention.

Esther and Benzy lived in Chicago, and in the 1930's, the Jewish quarter of Chicago had many *shtiblach*. In each of these, which were all located within a radius of a few blocks, there would be numerous *minyanim* (*minyan* is a quorum of ten, assembled for a public service), with services beginning at the crack of dawn and continuing well into the morning. By running back and forth among the *shtiblach*, catching each *minyan* at the recitation of *kedusha*, Esther was able to recite thirty-some *kedushas* every day!

Esther was a very short and fat woman, about as wide as she was tall. It was a sight to see this little figure rush hurriedly back and forth from *shtibl* to *shtibl* to make her quota of *kedushas*, thirty-some every day.

One might assume that with Esther heaping piles of curses on Benzy's head, their lives could hardly have been blissful. Why then did they keep the marriage going for sixty-five years? Why didn't they divorce?

Why don't elephants fly? Because they don't. The question is absurd. So is the question about Esther and Benzy divorcing. Although Jewish law provides for divorce, it just wasn't done. At least not for what was perceived as insignificant reasons, such as not "liking" each other.

But perhaps there was another reason over and above the social disapproval of divorce. Anger and bitterness are incompatible with gratitude. These emotions cannot co-exist in one person. Esther was far too busy running around saying *kedushas,* and expressing her thankfulness to God for giving her lovely and healthy children and grandchildren, to be able to harbor antithetical feelings of hostility.

I see some people today going through several marriages, disappointed and disillusioned with their previous relationships, searching for happiness and love, and apparently never finding it. Perhaps they would do better to run around for some *kedushas.*

❧

Father told me about how one particular marriage came about when two of our distant cousins, both simultaneously pregnant, decided that if one had a girl and the other a boy, they would enter into a marriage agreement.

The girl was born first. Several weeks later came a telegram, "Mazel Tov! Choson (bridegroom) born!"

The marriage took place many years later. However, whereas the young woman was exceedingly bright, the young man, albeit a hard-working *yeshiva bochur* (seminary student), was rather a dullard. His book-learning qualified him for *smicha* (ordination), and he received an appointment as Rabbi of a respectable Jewish community.

The wife had made peace with the marriage, since there was essentially no alternative. She knew that to be a successful rabbi required more than academic knowledge, which her husband rather lacked. She wanted to help him, yet knew that any overt assistance or intervention into his rabbinic duties on her part would be demeaning and would lower his self-esteem. She therefore used great caution and subtlety in helping her husband.

For example, she suggested to him that he never be quick to render a decision in a dispute. "Give yourself a chance to sleep on it. It's surprising about how a little time and pressure-free thinking can clarify things for you."

Most observant Jews took their business disputes to a rabbinic court rather than to the civil judiciary. When a case presented itself to the Rabbi, the wife would stand outside the study and overhear the proceedings.

That night at dinner she would say, "I heard some commotion coming from your study. I hope you don't mind my curiosity, but these things fascinate me. What was the problem?"

The Rabbi would respond, "Oh, Bronstein and Goldman are having a problem. They've been running a textile business for years and are now all entangled with conflicting claims to their respective shares."

The wife, who had already overheard all the detailed proceedings earlier in the day, would say, "Please don't get angry with me for being so nebby, but exactly what were they fighting about?"

"Well," the Rabbi would say, "they have been equal partners in the business. Now Bronstein wants to bring in his son and give him half of his share. Goldman is afraid that the young man is very aggressive and greedy, and feels threatened that he would be pushed out of the business. He says that Bronstein should buy him out, which Bronstein would be willing to do but doesn't have the money."

The wife would then say, "Oh, I see. Then your idea is for Bronstein to pay Goldman two thousand now, and give him a seventy per cent share of the profits for the next two years, and then Goldman is to leave the business completely, but continue to get ten percent of the profits for the next three years. Hmm! I like your idea. It's a bit complicated, but your solution just might be acceptable to everyone."

The Rabbi developed a reputation for handing down decisions of the caliber of Solomon's wisdom. Neither he nor anyone else ever knew that he had never formulated them, nor could he have. The desired goal was accomplished without jeopardizing the Rabbi's self-esteem.

Father would tell us that it is easy to help someone, but as meritorious as this might be, the recipient of help may feel humbled and downcast. It takes great effort and ingenuity to provide help in such a manner that the beneficiary's pride and self-esteem are preserved.

⁂

Moshe Mordcha was a little old man in his eighties. His second marriage to Chana had been a very happy one, but he couldn't think of too many pleasant things to say about his deceased first wife.

I was a yeshiva student at the time, and Moshe Mordcha assigned me the task of researching the theological authorities to see if anyone had stated what would happen, after resurrection of the dead, to a man who had remarried after being widowed. Obviously, monogamy was going to be retained, he had concluded. With both wives now alive, does one have to take the first wife, or does one have a choice? He dreaded the thought of having to surrender Chana and take his first wife back.

Alas! I could find nothing authoritative on the subject. Moshe Mordcha lived with the tormenting worry that resurrection might be disastrous.

◆

Father used to enjoy telling this one.

In days of yore, marriages were often arranged by the parents when the prospective bride and groom were yet children.

This occurred with the reknowned Reb Heschel, who was rabbi of Cracow in the seventeenth century, and who was a prodigy as a child.

One day Reb Heschel's father, a great Talmudist in his own right, called the young child into his study where a group of men were assembled. "Heschele," he said to the child of six, "I have just negotiated a *shiduch* (marriage match) for you. One of these men will be your father-in-law. Can you guess which one it is?

The child looked about the group and studied each individual, then singled out one person. "It is him," Reb Heschel said, guessing correctly, of course.

"Bravo!" everyone applauded. Then his father said, "Tell me, Heschele, how did you identify this man as your future father-in-law?"

"I looked at each person," the young child answered, "and when I came around to this man, I felt that for some reason I just could not stand him. So I knew he had to be the one."

◆

Of this same Reb Heschel, it is told that as a child, his father scolded him for not arising early in the morning to his Torah studies.

"I can't help it if I sleep late," the child said. "It is the Tempter's work. He tells me to turn over and sleep a bit more, and that it is yet too early to get up."

The father then said, "But, Heschele, don't you see? The Tempter is an angel created by God with a mission to divert people from observing and fulfilling the will of God. All the Tempter is doing is the job that he was assigned to do. So when the Tempter tells you to do something, such as not to get out of bed, you must reason, 'Aha! He is fulfilling *his* assignment. I, too, have a mission and an assignment which I must complete, and that is to pray and study Torah. Therefore, I must jump out of bed quickly to get on with *my* assignment.' "

"That's easy to say," the child responded. "But the Tempter has no difficulty in fulfilling his assignment, because he does not have a Tempter who is telling him to do otherwise, whereas I do."

❧

As a psychiatric resident, I was introduced to "projective techniques," to derive information about someone's unconscious thoughts. The best known of these is the Rorschach inkblot test, where a person is assumed to project his unconscious fantasies onto formless inkblots.

I recall that one of our congregants had a child who had night terrors. The child would wake up at night, screaming with fright, but no one knew what had frightened him. Old man Blum then offered to unravel the mystery.

The mother brought the child into one of the rooms adjacent to the *shul*. Blum took a large pan and filled it with cold water. He then put some beeswax into a saucepan and melted it on the stove. The mother held the pan of cold water over the child's head, and Blum poured the hot liquid beeswax into the pan of cold water. As the hot wax hit the cold water, it formed a flat amorphous glob, with many ridges and troughs. Blum then took the glob of wax and showed it to the child, asking, "What do you see here?" The child answered, "A dog." Blum then showed the glob of wax to the mother for her impression. The mother allowed that it might be a dog, but that it also looked like a Halloween mask.

Blum then came to the conclusion that the child had probably been frightened by a dog, or possibly by Halloween masqueraders who wore frightening masks. He suggested that the mother have the child play with a puppy, and take him to the candy store where the Halloween masks were sold, and let him play with some of these.

Blum made his living by peddling rags. He knew nothing of psychology, let alone Rorschach. Obviously, he had seen someone in the old country perform this procedure. It would be fascinating to know how many hundreds of years ago folk wisdom had developed the projective techniques.

❧

In the 1940's, Milwaukee had a centennial celebration, which featured a gala week of artistic performances by the country's leading virtuosos. One of these was the operatic tenor, Jan Peerce.

It so happened that the day of Peerce's appearance in

Milwaukee was the day of his father's *yahrzeit.* Peerce consulted the yellow pages for a *shul,* and went to a *shtibl,* where he was asked if he could lead the evening services.He was in great singing form, and the ten men who comprised the *minyan* were treated to a rare performance. Peerce treated every verse of the prayers as an aria.

The following morning Peerce came to the *minyan,* and again turned in a stellar performance. After the services, the *shul* president, Mr. Goldberg, gave Peerce three dollars. Peerce smiled and graciously refused.

A passerby who recognized Peerce as he left the shul went in and asked Goldberg, "What was Jan Peerce doing here?"

Goldberg shrugged his shoulders. "Peerce, shmeerce," he said. "He's a *chazan* (cantor) who is making the rounds looking for a job for Rosh Hoshanah. I wouldn't hire him. He's too loud. Hollers too much."

"Goldberg, you're an idiot," the man said. "That was Jan Peerce, the famous opera singer."

Goldberg appeared unimpressed. He had no idea what opera was nor who Peerce was.

"He's a *chazan'dl* looking for a position," Goldberg said. "I couldn't take him because he would make me a headache. Besides, with all his singing we wouldn't get out of *shul* until 5 o'clock. He's not for me. But he tried hard, so I gave him three dollars to help with his expenses. He refused the money; must have been insulted that I didn't give him more. But we are a small *shul* and can't afford to give more. Besides, he's not worth that much more. Hollers too much."

Never in Peerce's career were any of his critics as harsh on him as Goldberg.

Moshe and Chana were a rather unusual couple. The story I was told was that somehow Chana had been an old maid, unmarried at age 37, which was virtually unheard of in the old country. This was even more surprising because Chana came from an affluent family, and her generous dowry should have compensated for her physical unattractiveness. Chana's father became quite desperate to see her married, and when the matchmaker proposed Moshe to him, he readily accepted. Moshe had just turned eighteen, and as a result of his having been orphaned at a young age, not having received much of an education, and being without means or skills to support himself, he realized his chances of finding a more desirable match were very slim, and so the rather significant twenty-year age difference was not a deterrent to him.

Moshe and Chana lived out of town, and my mother did not know them. When they once visited our home, Mother almost committed the *faux pas* of chastising Moshe for not speaking more respectfully to his elderly *mother*. Fortunately, Father intervened just in time.

On coming to America, Moshe invested his money in a laundry and linen supply business, and built up a highly successful chain of laundries. However, he did not get much chance to enjoy his wealth, being in constant misery with severe stomach ulcers.

One time Moshe and Chaim came to visit my father. Chaim had hailed from the same Ukrainian village as Moshe, but his fortune had not been the same. He had managed to work himself up to a corner grocery, and was bewailing his plight to Moshe.

"I have to get up before dawn to get down to the market. From early morning until late at night, I stand on my feet waiting on customers and carrying heavy boxes. And when it is all over with, I have barely earned enough to eat decently. About all I can afford is a piece of dark bread, herring, and black radish for dinner," he complained.

"Chaim, you are a fool," Moshe responded. "Enjoy what you eat. I would gladly give away half of my laundries to be able to eat dark bread, herring, and black radish. What my ulcers let me eat is not worth eating."

The ways of God are unfathomable. Moshe died a young man, and Chana lived to almost one hundred, surviving him by thirty years.

❧

If all marriages are made in Heaven, I find it difficult to understand the reasoning of the angels in pairing up Zalman with Malka.

Malka was a highly refined woman, very quiet, gentle, and always caring for others. Zalman was a boor, and his behavior was often vulgar and uncouth. These two lived together for over fifty years.

What held them together? For all his boorishness, Zalman had some appreciation for Malka. Sure, he was critical when she gave away much of the house money for charity, but he continued to supply her, knowing she would give it away. Perhaps he felt that he had little merit of his own, and that Malka would be his ticket to Heaven.

But why did Malka stay with Zalman? It was distressing to watch her blush with embarrassment when Zalman would make one of his crude, tasteless remarks at a social gathering. She would try to right things, but it was clear that she would have been relieved if the ground had opened and just swallowed her. Yet, Malka was a devoted wife.

I remember one time when their son rented a small shop which he was going to use to purchase rags and scrap metal from peddlers. The shop was located on a block where another man had been operating a similar business for years.

When Zalman found out about this, he told his son to get rid of the shop, because he had no right to open a competing business right under another person's nose. "Get yourself another place a few blocks away," he said. "You don't open a competing business where you are likely to draw away someone else's clients."

The son explained that it was too late. He had already signed a two-year lease for the shop, and he stood to lose a great deal of money if he breached the contract.

"I don't give a damn what you signed and how much you will lose. If you open that shop on the same block, I will break every bone in your body. You can make a living someplace else and God will help you. But you can't expect His help if you interfere with someone else's livelihood," Zalman said.

The competing shop was never opened.

I can conceive that many sophisticated and highly polished people might not have taken this stand. They might have had the capacity to rationalize and justify what Zalman's son was doing. After all, isn't competition what free enterprise is all about?

Zalman was a boor. He couldn't rationalize, so he knew what was unethical when he saw it. Perhaps Malka knew Zalman better than we did.

XIII
At the Close

Father continued to teach us to enjoy life until the end, the very end.

During his terminal illness, Father told us that in the year following his death, if there were any occasion for celebration within the family — wedding, Bar-Mitzvah, birth — he wished that all mourning be suspended, and for everyone to rejoice to the utmost. He felt that after the first thirty days, during which mourning was obligatory, he had the right to dispense of restrictions which were in his honor.

Father instructed us individually, but one request he made of all of us was that we do not follow the tradition of naming a newborn child after him. To me he said that although he dearly loved all his grandchildren, he nevertheless felt himself to be partial to those who bore his mother's name. He felt that it was not fair to other children to bestow a most-favored status on one.

To my brother, however, Father offered another reason. "I have often arbitrated between a couple," he said, "when a child was born and the father and mother each wished to name the child after a member of his or her family, respectively. I have seen totally unnecessary and senseless suffering result from the desire to perpetuate the memory of a relative by the naming of a child. I do not want a young mother, who should be rejoicing with her newborn child, to cry herself to sleep because one of *my* children, insisting that the child bear *my* name, was frustrating her wish to name the child after her relative."

Why was a different reason given to my brother? Could it have been because several years later, shortly after his wife's father died, he might have otherwise found himself in a conflict with his wife over which grandfather's name should be given to their newborn child? Do people have such prophetic foresight?

Father died on the day following *Tisha B'Av,* the day of national mourning for the destruction of the *Bet Hamikdosh* (Sanctuary in Jerusalem). Of course, the *yahrzeit* occurs on that day each year. It is as though Father felt that since mourning would be inevitable, the least one could do is to attach it to a pre-existing obligatory day of mourning, rather than allow the normal flow of joyous living to be interrupted.

Perhaps the latter occurence was Father's unspoken and unconscious prayer. With the last act of his life, he again emphasized his creed, *Lebedig, kinderlach, Lebedig.*

XIV
Glossary

Ahavas Yisroel — love for a fellow Jew
Amidah — the 19-paragraph prayer recited three times daily, in an upright posture
Aron hakodesh — ark containing the Torah scrolls
Chaver — friend, companion
Chazan — cantor
Chazer — pork
Chometz — bread or any leavened dough product
Dayan — magistrate, judge
Esrog — a species of citrus fruit, used ritually on *Sukkos*
Fleishig — containing meat or meat products
Goy — non-Jew, gentile
Hachnosas kalah — providing means for an indigent girl to marry
Haggadah — narrative of the Exodus from Egypt, recited at the Passover Seder
Hakafah — procession around the altar
Halacha — Jewish law, as elaborated in the Talmud and codified in the Shulchan Aruch; lit., the going
Kedusha — sanctity, holiness; also refers to a prayer in the amidah
Kiddush — prayer inaugurating *Shabbos* or one of the holidays, usually recited over wine

Kiddush hashem — lit., sanctifying the divine name, often refering to martyrdom
Kugel — a kind of pudding
Kvittel — a slip of paper containing one's requests, submitted to a Rebbe as a petition
Lashon hara — gossip, slander
L'chayim — traditional toast; lit., "to life"
Lulav — a palm branch, used ritually together with the *esrog* on *Sukkos*
Meschuga — insane
Meshumed — a convert from Judaism to another religion
Michuten — parents of one's son-in-law or daughter-in-law
Mikva — pool for ritual immersion
Milchig — containing milk or dairy products
Mincha — afternoon prayer
Minyan — quorum of ten adult males
Mishna — earliest portion of the Talmud
Mitzva — lit., a divine commandment; colloquially, any good deed
Mizrach — east; also refers to a plaque identifying east
Nachas — pleasure and enjoyment, often referring to that derived from one's children and grandchildren
Neshama — soul
N'velah — meat not ritually slaughtered
Pidyon haben — ceremony of redemption of the firstborn
Poritz — feudal lord
Rosh Hashana — New Year
Schmaltz — chicken fat
Schnorrer — beggar, moocher
Seder — the meal of the first two nights of Passover
Selichos — prayers for forgiveness
Shamas — beadle
Shechina — presence of the Divine spirit

Shema Yisrael — prayer declaring the unity of God
Shiduch — a marriage match
Shmata — rag
Shochet — ritual slaughterer, butcher
Shtibel — small synagogue
Shul — synagogue
Sidur — prayer book; lit., order
Simcha — joy or happiness; also used to refered to a joyous occasion
Sukka — a small hut with thatched roof, used as a temporary dwelling during *Sukkos*
Sukkos — the eight day Feast of Tabernacles
Talis — prayer shawl
Talis koton — a four-cornered garment with tzitzis, worn by men
Talmud — body of laws and ethics compiled between 200 B.C.E. and 400 C.E.
Tfillin — leather phylacteries, containing portions of the scriptures, used in daily morning prayer
T'hillim — Psalms
Tisha B'Av — Ninth day of the month of Av, commemorating the destruction of both sanctuaries in Jerusalem
Trefa — forbidden food
Tshuva — repentance
Tzdaka — alms, charity
Tzuris — troubles
Yeshiva bochur — seminary student
Yom Kippur — Day of Atonement
Yom tov — holiday; lit., good day
Zaddik — a just or pious person; also used to refer to a person of outstanding saintliness. Among chassidim, zaddik is often a synonym for "Rebbe"
Zeide — grandfather, ancestor